MELTED CHEESE

MELTED CHEESE

60 gorgeously gooey recipes

RYLAND PETERS & SMALL

LONDON • NEW YORK

Senior Designer Toni Kay
Senior Editor Abi Waters
Production Manager Gordana Simakovic
Art Director Leslie Harrington
Editorial Director Julia Charles

Indexer Vanessa Bird

First published in 2024 by
Ryland Peters & Small
20–21 Jockey's Fields, London WC1R 4BW
and
341 E 116th St, New York NY 10029
www.rylandpeters.com

10 9 8 7 6 5 4 3 2 1

Text copyright © Fiona Beckett, Maxine Clark,
Megan Davies, Ross Dobson, Tori Haschka, Lizzie
Kamenetzky, Kathy Kordalis, Jenny Linford, Claire
McDonald & Lucy McDonald, Hannah Miles,
Louise Pickford, Fiona Smith, Jenny Tschiesche,
Laura Washburn Hutton, Belinda Williams and
Ryland Peters & Small 2024

Design and photographs copyright © Ryland
Peters & Small 2024

ISBN: 978-1-78879-647-7

Printed in China

A CIP record for this book is available from
the British Library.

US Library of Congress Cataloging-in-Publication
Data has been applied for.

NOTES:
• Both British (Metric) and American (Imperial
plus US cups) measurements are included in
these recipes for your convenience, however it is
important to work with one set of measurements
and not alternate between the two within a recipe.
• All spoon measurements are level unless
otherwise specified.
• All eggs are medium (UK) or large (US), unless
specified as large, in which case US extra-large
should be used. Uncooked or partially cooked
eggs should not be served to the very old, frail,
young children, pregnant women or those with
compromised immune systems.
• Ovens should be preheated to the specified
temperatures. We recommend using an oven
thermometer. If using a fan-assisted oven, adjust
temperatures according to the manufacturer's
instructions.
• When a recipe calls for the grated zest of
citrus fruit, buy unwaxed fruit and wash well
before using. If you can only find treated fruit,
scrub well in warm soapy water before using.

CONTENTS

INTRODUCTION

Perfect for making a big night in an indulgent experience to remember, this book features 60 decadent recipes just oozing with melted golden goodness. From grilled cheese sandwiches, designed for gorging on all alone, to big pots of fondue for sharing with friends, there is no shame in enjoying melted cheese for one, but equally it is good to share the love, too. In these pages, you'll discover a multitude of ways to serve your favourite comfort food in various delicious guises.

It is no coincidence that some of the most-loved dishes from all over the world include melted cheese in one form or another. Switzerland has given us fondue and raclette, Italy offers cheese-loaded pizza and pasta and Mexican cuisine brings nachos and enchiladas to the party. British favourites include Welsh rarebit and cauliflower cheese, and who could forget the all-American cheeseburger or mac 'n' cheese? Of course, we all now mix and match these melted cheese favourites all over the world and make our own variations on these popular dishes. No matter how many evolutions they seem go through, the one common theme – copious amounts of melted cheese – stays the same!

But why are we so captivated by this alluring foodstuff to the point of cultural obsession? It could be the way it goes stringy when you take a big bite, or the way it bubbles and turns golden when you remove it from the oven. Maybe it's the creamy texture coupled with the unique savoury taste, or the type of warm, comforting, carby dishes it goes on. Whatever it is, our age-old love affair with melted cheese shows no signs of slowing.

A BRIEF HISTORY OF MELTED CHEESE

It's near on impossible to pinpoint the moment in history that people discovered smothering food in melted cheese to be an excellent idea. The discovery of a basic early form of cheese is thought to have occurred around 8,000 BC. It probably occurred by accident, in a country with a warm climate, when milk was transported inside animal membranes. These membranes contain natural enzymes that would eventually turn the milk into cheese.

Making cheese began to be considered something of an art-form in the Roman era, and it was served to the rich. The cheeses that we are familiar with today began to be produced in the cooler climate of Europe in the Middle Ages. The first cheese factory was constructed in 1815 in Switzerland, and once scientists discovered how to pasteurize it, mass production of cheese sky-rocketed worldwide. Processed American cheese was invented around 1910 and became a hit because it melts so well. The cheeseburger is said to have been invented in America in 1926 and fondue was popularized as a Swiss national dish by the Swiss Cheese Union in the 1930s. In more recent decades, hand-made artisan cheeses have become favoured, as people have discovered how best to cook with and flavour-match the various types available.

THE SCIENCE BEHIND MELTED CHEESE

Cheese itself is usually an emulsion of dairy fat and water, bound together by proteins. But different cheeses have different additional ingredients and different ratios of fat and water, and therefore have differing optimum melting points. The first stage of melting occurs in most cheeses about 32°C (90°F), where the milk fat starts to soften. The cheese may start to 'sweat' or become pliable. As heat increases, the protein bonds break down too and the whole thing completely collapses into a gooey puddle.

The things that affect how a cheese melts:
- *moisture content*
- *fat content*
- *acidity content*
- *age*

Softer cheeses with a high moisture content melt completely at around 54°C (130°F), for aged lower-moisture cheeses it's 65°C (150°F) and hard, dry cheeses need to reach up to about 82°C (180°F). Generally speaking, the higher the moisture content, the better the melt. The increased water content allows cheeses to completely liquefy.

Cheeses loaded with fat make perfect melters (just one reason why full-fat cheese is always preferable) and cheeses with naturally occurring acid are able to dissolve more easily under heat. Finally, cheeses that are more aged sometimes have a tougher time melting as the proteins become more tightly bound.

TIPS & TRICKS FOR MELTING CHEESE LIKE A PRO

Granted, some cheeses melt more easily than others, but, as a cook, there are still definitely things you can do to make sure your melted cheese is the best it can possibly be.

Pick the right cheese for the right recipe

Different cheeses respond to heat in different ways. Some become liquid, some become stringy and some just soften or don't really melt at all. It's fine to mix and match the cheeses in these recipes, just make sure you refer to the guide on page 10 to help you pick something that is right for your recipe.

Choose your cooking method wisely

The oven is a great way to melt cheese because it provides a nice even heat and you can easily control the temperature. Alternatively, the grill/broiler is perfect for turning cheesy toppings golden. It is not a good idea to melt cheese in the microwave, as the uneven heat will leave some bits of cheese scalding hot and others lukewarm and not fully melted.

Treat it gently

Melting cheese requires a delicate touch. Don't stir too roughly when making cheese sauces and don't heat your cheese too quickly at a fierce temperature. Heating cheese too fiercely can sometimes result in its proteins separating from the water and fat rather than nicely emulsifying, leaving you with rubbery cheese and pools of oil. This is at worst a bit disappointing on a pizza, but it's a full-blown disaster in a cheese sauce or a fondue.

Bring it to room temperature first

If it's fridge-cold all the way through, your cheese will take longer to break down. Bringing it to room temperature before cooking gives it a head start and lessens the dramatic rapid change in temperature, which could result in the liquid and fat separation.

Grate/shred it

Grating or shredding cheese that is going to be melted is a wise move, as it gives more surface area for the heat to permeate and thus the melting process will be quicker. It also means you will have perfectly even pieces, which will all melt as the same rate.

A cheese plane slicer is also a great tool for making thin, evenly sized slices of cheese ready for melting.

Acidity and starch are your friends

Certain ingredients can affect the texture of melted cheese. White wine or lemon juice are both acidic and can be added to fondues, sauces or soups to help keep the texture silky smooth. Starches such as flour or cornflour/cornstarch also act as a barrier against clumps.

Keep it hot

If you let melted cheese cool too much before serving, it will lose its beautiful oozing texture and become firm and congealed. Serve immediately for best results.

Use processed cheese for a fail-safe option

Processed cheese is a quick and easy melter – it has a low melting point and, no matter how much you overheat it, will stay smooth and flowing. It might not have the best flavour, but it's great on things like barbecued/grilled burgers where you can't control the fierce heat as easily.

WHICH CHEESES MELT BEST?

Mozzarella With a very high moisture content, mozzarella melts quickly and easily. It is famous for its amazing 'pull' – the long stringy, stretchy bits. With a mild, creamy taste it is a great 'topper' but doesn't work as well in soups or sauces. Try it on pizza or pasta, with meatballs or in grilled cheese sandwiches.

Cheddar A go-to option for lovers of melted cheese, this all-rounder works in pretty much everything. The sharper and more aged the cheese, the more heat it will need to melt. Try it in soups, béchamel sauces, toasties or burgers.

Gruyère High in acid, this cheese is favoured for its smooth melt, as well as its salty-sweet-nutty taste. It is one of the Alpine cheeses and is perfect in fondue, for topping French onion soup or for adding to gratins.

Camembert This cheese is a king among melters. It goes exceptionally creamy and most people prefer to serve it straight-up out of the box, with crudités or crusty bread for dipping.

Brie With a very high moisture and fat content, this is another excellent melter. Try it in sandwiches or burgers. It goes exceptionally well with bacon and piquant condiments.

Fontina This buttery and mildly tangy Italian cheese turns into a tasty oozy mess when melted. Good in sandwiches and for topping potatoes; remember to remove the rind first.

Raclette The word raclette is the name of an incredible Swiss cheese and the dish you use it for. To serve raclette at home, you will need to invest in a raclette grill (see page 123).

CHAPTER 1
SOUPS & SANDWICHES

BROCCOLI & BLUE CHEESE SOUP

Mrs Bells Blue is a soft blue British cheese by Shepherds Purse Cheeses. You can use any mid-strength blue cheese as an alternative.

50 g/3½ tbsp unsalted butter
6 banana shallots, finely chopped
3 potatoes, peeled and finely chopped
4 celery sticks/ribs, sliced
1.5 litres/6 cups chicken stock
950 g/2 lbs. 2 oz. purple sprouting or new-season tender broccoli
400 g/14 oz. Mrs Bells Blue or other creamy blue cheese, such as Stilton
pinch of grated nutmeg
200 ml/¾ cup double/heavy cream
freshly ground black pepper
croutons, to serve

SERVES 6

Melt the butter in a large saucepan, add the shallots and cook gently for a few minutes to soften. Add the potatoes and celery, and stir to coat well with the butter. Add the stock and bring the liquid to the boil, then simmer for 15–20 minutes until the potato is almost tender.

Add the broccoli and continue to cook for a further 3–5 minutes until the stalks are tender. It is crucial not to overcook the broccoli or you lose the lovely bright green colour.

Purée the soup immediately with a blender. When smooth, crumble in three-quarters of the blue cheese, and add a pinch of nutmeg and a good twist of black pepper to season. Stir in almost all of the cream, reserving a little to garnish.

Ladle the soup into bowls, garnish with a swirl of cream and crumble over the remaining blue cheese. Serve immediately, with croutons.

FRENCH ONION SOUP WITH COMTÉ TOASTS

Molten Comté, with its nutty, earthy taste and creamy texture, is the ideal choice for these oozing toasts that soak up the rich broth of the onion soup to perfection.

30 g/2 tbsp unsalted butter
3 tbsp olive oil
1 kg/2 lb. 4 oz. large onions,
    very thinly sliced
250 ml/1 cup dry white wine
1 litre/4 cups rich beef stock
good pinch of grated nutmeg
small handful of fresh thyme sprigs
2 fresh bay leaves
75 ml/⅓ cup good-quality Madeira
1 day-old baguette or other
    crusty bread, cut into slices
1 garlic clove, peeled
150 g/5½ oz. Comté, grated/shredded
salt and black pepper

SERVES 4

Melt the butter in a heavy-based pan or flameproof casserole dish and add the oil. Add the onions and season with salt. Cook over low heat, stirring occasionally, for at least 45 minutes until they have reduced right down to a golden, sticky mass.

Add the wine and bubble, stirring, for a minute, then add the beef stock, a good grating of nutmeg and the herbs. Simmer for about 20 minutes, then add the Madeira and bubble for 5 minutes more. Check the seasoning and spoon into four small ovenproof bowls or dishes.

Preheat the grill/broiler to high.

Toast the slices of crusty bread and rub one side all over with the garlic. Put the toasts on top of the bowls so that they cover the surface of the soup. Sprinkle with lots and lots of cheese and put on a baking sheet under the grill/broiler until the soup is bubbling and the cheese toasts are melted and golden. Serve straight away.

BROWN BUTTER BAKED POTATO SOUP

Rich and creamy with sour cream and grated cheese, this is a perfect comforting soup for cold winter days.

4 large baking potatoes
110 g/½ cup/1 stick unsalted butter
1 litre/4 cups chicken or
    vegetable stock
150 ml/⅔ cup sour cream
130 g/4½ oz. Cheddar,
    grated/shredded
olive oil, to drizzle
salt and black pepper

SERVES 4

Preheat the oven to 200°C (400°F) Gas 6.

Prick the potatoes with a fork, rub the skins with a little salt and bake in the preheated oven for about 1 hour until the potatoes are soft when you insert a sharp knife into the centre. Set aside until cool enough to handle without burning yourself.

In a saucepan, melt the butter over gentle heat until it starts to brown lightly – the butter will smell nutty, which is how you will know it is ready. Scoop out the potato from the skins (reserving the skins for the garnish) and add to the butter. Cook for a few minutes, then add the stock and simmer for 5–10 minutes. Add the sour cream and 100 g/3½ oz. of the grated cheese, then blitz the soup in a blender or food processor until smooth (or use a stick blender). Pour the soup back into the saucepan, season with salt and pepper to taste and keep warm.

Preheat the grill/broiler to high. Place the reserved potato skins on a baking sheet and drizzle with a little olive oil. Sprinkle with the remaining 30 g/1 oz. grated cheese and season with salt and pepper. Place under the hot grill and grill/broil until the cheese has melted and the skins are crispy – this will take about 5 minutes, but watch them carefully as grills are all different and you don't want them to burn.

Serve the soup in bowls with a drizzle of olive oil and the crispy potato skins broken up on top or served whole on the side.

FIELD MUSHROOM SOUP
WITH PARMESAN, THYME & BACON

The earthy field mushrooms in this delicious soup pair perfectly with the rich bacon, herby thyme and salty Parmesan. Always feel free to add extra cheese, if liked, too!

100 g/7 tbsp unsalted butter
1 onion, finely chopped
1 garlic clove, crushed
6 small waxy potatoes, peeled and finely chopped
8 large flat field mushrooms, sliced
800 ml/3⅓ cups vegetable stock
a muslin/cheesecloth bag filled with bay leaves and a few juniper berries, sprigs of thyme and black peppercorns, tied with string/twine
150 ml/⅔ cup double/heavy cream, plus extra to serve
a dollop of Dijon mustard, to taste
150 g/5½ oz. dry-cured bacon, cooked until crispy and cut into long pieces
50 g/1¾ oz. Parmesan, grated/shredded
fresh thyme leaves, to garnish

SERVES 6

Melt the butter in a large saucepan, add the onion, garlic and potatoes, and cook until the onion is softened, but do not allow to brown. Add the field mushrooms and toss around until they start to wilt. (Mushrooms are very greedy with butter and tend to suck it all up while they are deciding to cook, then spit it all out again when they have relented to soften. If you have yourself some particularly greedy mushrooms, you may need to add a little more butter.)

When the mushrooms have eventually settled down and reduced in size, add the stock. Add your muslin bag of infusion, cover the pan and turn the heat down to a very low simmer. Somehow the longer this cooks, the better it is; mushrooms are fussy creatures and do not like being rushed!

When the flavours have married – this should take about 40 minutes – remove from the heat and remove the muslin bag. Stir in the cream and mustard, then blend with a stick blender until smooth.

Serve the soup in big rustic bowls with a swirl of cream to contrast against the dark grey of the mushrooms. Top with the bacon pieces and a sprinkling of Parmesan, then garnish with a few fresh thyme leaves.

CAULIFLOWER & GRUYÈRE SOUP

Try and find a small, whole head of cauliflower that is creamy-white and soft for this gorgeously cheesy soup.

30 g/2 tbsp unsalted butter
1 onion, roughly chopped
1 celery stick/rib, chopped
1 small cauliflower, about 1 kg/
    2 lb. 4 oz., cut into small pieces
1.5 litres/6 cups vegetable or
    chicken stock
250 ml/1 cup double/heavy cream
200 g/7 oz. Gruyère, grated/shredded,
    plus extra to garnish
salt and black pepper
freshly chopped parsley, to garnish
toasted wholemeal bread, to serve

SERVES 4

Heat the butter in a saucepan over high heat. Add the onion and celery and cook for about 5 minutes until the onion has softened but not browned.

Add the cauliflower pieces and stock, and bring to the boil. Continue to boil for 25–30 minutes until the cauliflower is really soft and breaking up in the stock.

Transfer the mixture to a food processor or blender and process the mixture in batches until smooth. Return the purée to a clean saucepan. Add the cream and cheese, and cook over low heat, stirring constantly, until the cheese has all smoothly melted into the soup. Season to taste with a little salt and black pepper.

Serve sprinkled with chopped parsley and extra cheese to garnish, and with buttered wholemeal toast on the side.

SPINACH & PARMESAN SOUP
WITH NUTMEG & ROSEMARY

This recipe uses the robust flavour of Parmesan, but any other hard, strong cheese would do instead. You can use the tender, washed bags of spinach we find in our grocery stores or a tougher variety such as epinard, with the tough stalks trimmed away.

50 g/3½ tbsp unsalted butter
6 strong shallots, chopped
2 garlic cloves, crushed
1 large potato, peeled and finely chopped
2 tbsp chopped fresh rosemary leaves,
    plus extra sprigs to garnish
1.5 litres/6 cups chicken stock
1 kg/2 lbs. 4 oz. spinach leaves,
    any really coarse stalks removed
    and chopped to a manageable size
pinch of grated nutmeg, plus extra
    to garnish
200 g/7 oz. Parmesan, or other hard
    strong cheese, grated/shredded
crème fraîche or sour cream, to taste
salt and black pepper

SERVES 6–8

In a large saucepan, melt the butter, then add the shallots and garlic, and cook gently for a few minutes until softened.

Add the potato and rosemary, cover with the stock and bring to a simmer. Cook for 15–20 minutes until the potato is tender.

Add the spinach to the pan and bring to the boil, then remove the pan from the heat and blend well with a stick blender.

Add a pinch of grated nutmeg, and season well with salt and pepper. Stir in the Parmesan and a few tablespoons of crème fraîche to enrich the soup to your taste.

Serve with an extra spoonful of crème fraîche and garnish with a dusting of nutmeg and a few sprigs of fresh rosemary.

BASIC GRILLED CHEESE

This is the basic grilled cheese method, which can be used as a blueprint for all sorts of experimentation. It's a good idea to start with two relatively mild cheeses, such as a mild Cheddar and Monterey Jack.

4 large slices white bread
unsalted butter, softened
300 g/10½ oz. mixed mild cheeses,
    such as mild Cheddar, Gruyére,
    Monterey Jack or Gouda,
    grated/shredded

SERVES 2

Butter each of the bread slices on one side.

Without turning the heat on, place two slices of the bread in a large, non-stick frying pan/skillet, butter-side down. If you can only accommodate one slice in your pan, you'll need to cook one sandwich at a time. Top each slice with half of the grated cheese, but be careful not to let too much cheese fall into the pan. Top with the final pieces of bread, butter-side up.

Turn the heat to medium and cook for 3–4 minutes on the first side, then carefully turn with a large spatula and cook on the second side for 2–3 minutes until the sandwiches are golden all over and all the cheese is visibly melted.

Remove from the pan and cut the sandwiches in half. Let cool for a few minutes before serving. These are lovely served with a steaming bowl of tomato soup for dunking.

THE ULTIMATE CHEESE TOASTIE

What makes a good cheese toastie? This toastie starts in a frying pan/skillet and finishes in the oven, ensuring a crisp toasted crust and an evenly soft and gooey centre. Use good-quality mustard, cheese and ham.

150 g/5½ oz. aged Gruyère, finely grated/shredded
1 tbsp dry white wine
3 tbsp crème fraîche or sour cream
65 g/4½ tbsp unsalted butter, softened
4 slices sourdough or rustic white bread
1 tbsp Dijon mustard
2 thick slices good-quality cooked ham
freshly ground black pepper
pickles, to serve

SERVES 2

Preheat the oven to 190°C (375°F) Gas 5.

Combine the Gruyère, wine, crème fraîche and some pepper to make a paste. Butter one side of each piece of bread, followed by a little mustard. Place two of the slices mustard side-up on a board. Spread half of the cheese paste over the mustard, top with the ham, then the remaining paste. Top with the remaining slices of bread, mustard-side down, and press together.

Melt the remaining butter in an ovenproof frying pan/skillet over medium–low heat, add the sandwiches and cook for a minute on each side until lightly golden. Transfer the pan to the preheated oven and bake for 10 minutes until golden, gooey and yummy. Serve with pickles.

RED ONION CHUTNEY & CHEDDAR TOASTIE

Cheddar and chutney is a winning combination, but for best results, be sure to use a really gutsy mature Cheddar here. The chutney needs to have a good balance of sweetness and tartness to make this work perfectly, so be sure to taste and adjust before assembling the sandwiches.

4 slices white bread
unsalted butter, softened
150 g/5½ oz. mature/sharp Cheddar, grated/shredded

QUICK CHUTNEY
2 tbsp vegetable oil
2 red onions, halved and thinly sliced
good pinch of salt
1 tbsp light soft brown sugar
2 tbsp wine vinegar
2 tbsp balsamic vinegar

SERVES 2

For the chutney, heat the oil in small non-stick frying pan/skillet, add the onions and cook over medium–high heat, stirring occasionally, until caramelized. Add the remaining chutney ingredients, reduce to a simmer and cook until sticky but still somewhat liquid. Taste and adjust the seasoning, adding more sugar for sweetness or vinegar for tartness, as required.

Butter each of the bread slices on one side and set aside.

Without turning the heat on, place two slices of bread in a large, ridged griddle/stove-top pan, butter-side down. If you can fit only one slice in your pan, you'll need to cook one sandwich at a time. Spread generously with some of the chutney and sprinkle each slice with half the grated cheese in an even layer. Cover with another bread slice, butter-side up.

Turn the heat to medium and cook for 3–4 minutes until a deep golden colour, pressing gently with a spatula. Carefully turn with the spatula and cook on the second side for 2–3 minutes, or until deep golden brown all over. To achieve the lovely criss-cross pattern, turn the sandwiches over again, rotate them 90° to the left or right, and cook for a final 2–3 minutes.

Remove from the pan, transfer to a plate and cut in half. Let cool for a few minutes before serving with extra chutney.

LEEK & GRUYÈRE GRILLED CHEESE

A strong French Gruyère melts beautifully and is certainly up there among the finest of cheeses. If a grilled cheese sandwich could be French, it would be this one – simple yet elegant. Serve with a glass of chilled white wine.

4 slices white bread
unsalted butter, softened
wholegrain Dijon mustard
250 g/9 oz. Gruyère, grated/shredded

LEEKS

1 large leek, thinly sliced into rounds
1 tsp vegetable oil
15 g/1 tbsp unsalted butter
½ tsp dried thyme
6 tbsp dry white wine
salt and black pepper

SERVES 2

For the leeks, in a non-stick frying pan/skillet, combine the leek, oil, butter and thyme over medium–high heat and cook, stirring occasionally, until soft and golden. Season well, add the wine and simmer until the liquid evaporates. Taste and adjust the seasoning. Set aside.

Butter each of the bread slices on one side, then spread two of the slices with mustard on the non-buttered side.

Without turning the heat on, place two slices of the bread in a large, ridged griddle/stove-top pan, butter-side down. If you can only fit one slice in your pan, you'll need to cook one sandwich at a time. Spoon half of the leek mixture over each slice and sprinkle over half the grated cheese in an even layer. Cover with another bread slice each, mustard-side down.

Turn the heat to medium and cook the first side for 3–5 minutes until it turns a deep golden colour, pressing gently with a spatula. Carefully turn with the spatula and cook on the second side for 2–3 minutes, or until deep golden brown all over.

Remove from the pan, transfer to a plate and cut the sandwiches in half. Let cool for a few minutes before serving.

MUSHROOM & FONTINA TOASTIE

Here, tangy balsamic mushrooms offer an earthy accompaniment to the rich melted Fontina. Like most grilled cheese sandwiches, this one goes well with tomato soup, but also works nicely with a hearty cream of mushroom soup.

4 slices granary/granary-style bread
unsalted butter, softened
150g/5½ oz. Fontina, grated/shredded or thinly sliced

MUSHROOMS
30 g/2 tbsp unsalted butter
1 tbsp vegetable oil
125 g/1⅓ cups white mushrooms, thinly sliced
1 shallot, finely chopped
½ tsp dried thyme
3 tbsp balsamic vinegar
1 tsp red wine vinegar
salt and black pepper

SERVES 2

For the mushrooms, in a non-stick frying pan/skillet, combine the butter, oil, mushrooms, shallot and thyme over medium–high heat and cook, stirring occasionally, until everything is soft and deep golden in colour. Season well, add the vinegars and simmer until the liquid almost evaporates. Taste and adjust the seasoning.

Butter each of the bread slices on one side.

Without turning the heat on, place two slices of the bread in a large, non-stick frying pan, butter-side down. If you can only fit one slice in your pan, you'll need to cook one sandwich at a time. Spoon over half of the mushrooms and sprinkle half of the grated cheese on top in an even layer. Cover each slice with another bread slice, butter-side up.

Turn the heat to medium and cook the first side for 3–5 minutes until it turns a deep golden colour, pressing gently with a spatula. Carefully turn with the spatula and cook on the second side for 2–3 minutes, or until deep golden brown all over.

Remove from the frying pan, transfer to a plate and cut the sandwiches in half. Let cool for a few minutes before serving.

BRIE & APPLE-CRANBERRY TOASTIE

Thin slices of Brie melt more successfully than thick ones, so a good tip is to remove the rind and slice the cheese when it is chilled (which is easier), then bring the slices to room temperature before using in the sandwich.

4–8 slices walnut bread, depending on size of loaf

unsalted butter, softened

180g/6 oz. ripe chilled Brie, rind removed, thinly sliced

APPLE-CRANBERRY SAUCE

300 g/3 cups cranberries, fresh or frozen

juice of 1 orange

1 small tart cooking apple, such as Cox, peeled and finely chopped

3 tbsp caster/granulated sugar, or to taste

SERVES 2

For the apple-cranberry sauce, combine all the ingredients in a saucepan over low heat. Stir until the sugar dissolves and the cranberries begin to pop and disintegrate. If the mixture is too dry, add a small amount of water. Cover and simmer gently until the cranberries are tender and the mixture has a jam-like consistency; if the mixture is too dry, add a little water to prevent the mixture from thickening and burning. Taste and adjust the sweetness to your liking. Set aside until needed.

Butter the bread slices on one side.

Without turning the heat on, place two slices of the bread in a large, heavy-based, non-stick frying pan/skillet, butter-side down. If you can't fit two slices side-by-side in the pan, you'll need to cook them in two batches. Spread the slices generously with some of the apple-cranberry sauce, then top with Brie slices. Cover with the remaining bread slices, butter-side up.

Turn the heat to medium and cook the first side for 3–5 minutes until it turns a deep golden colour, pressing gently with a spatula. Carefully turn with the spatula and cook on the second side for 2–3 minutes, or until deep golden brown all over.

Remove from the frying pan, transfer to a plate and cut in half. Let cool for a few minutes before serving along with extra apple-cranberry sauce.

PUTTANESCA & MOZZARELLA FOCACCIA

Halfway between a pizza and a pasta sauce, this sandwich brings together classic Italian ingredients. Fresh mozzarella melts best, so be sure to use this if you can and you'll be in for a real treat.

large round or square focaccia, halved lengthways and widthways

extra-virgin olive oil, for brushing

4 tbsp black olive paste

2 tbsp sun-dried tomato paste

4–6 tbsp passata/strained tomatoes

2 mozzarella balls, drained and thinly sliced

2 tsp dried oregano

2 tbsp grated/shredded Parmesan

2–3 tbsp capers, drained

good pinch of dried chilli/hot red pepper flakes

few fresh basil leaves, torn

SERVES 2–4

Brush the outsides of the focaccia halves with olive oil and arrange oil-side down on a clean board.

Spread two of the non-oiled sides generously with the olive paste. Spread the other two non-oiled sides with the sun-dried tomato paste, then top with the passata. Divide the mozzarella slices between the tomato-coated sides. Sprinkle over the oregano, Parmesan, capers and chilli flakes. Scatter over a few basil leaves. Top with the olive oil-coated bread, oil-side up.

Without turning the heat on, place the sandwiches in a large, non-stick frying pan/skillet. If you can fit only one sandwich in your pan, you'll need to cook one sandwich at a time.

Turn the heat to medium and cook the first side for 4–5 minutes, then carefully turn with a large spatula and cook the other side for 2–3 minutes, pressing down gently with the spatula until golden brown all over.

Remove from the frying pan, transfer to a wooden chopping board or a plate and cut the sandwiches in half. Let cool for a few minutes before serving.

KIMCHI & MONTEREY JACK TOASTIE

Melted cheese is complemented by sour or tangy ingredients that cut through the richness. Here, kimchi, a spiced Korean condiment of fermented pickled cabbage, does just that to perfection. The combination may sound strange at first, but it's fantastic. There's a good reason why kimchi is taking off around the world!

4 slices white bread, crusts removed
unsalted butter, softened
60 g/½ cup kimchi
150 g/5½ oz. mild cheese, such as Monterey Jack or mild Cheddar, grated/shredded

SERVES 2

Butter each of the bread slices on one side and set aside.

Pat the kimchi dry with paper towels to remove excess moisture and chop.

Without turning the heat on, put two slices of the bread in a large, heavy-based non-stick frying pan/skillet, butter-side down. If you can fit only one slice in your pan, you'll need to cook one sandwich at a time. Top with half the kimchi and sprinkle over half the grated cheese in an even layer. Cover each with another bread slice, butter-side up.

Turn the heat to medium and cook the first side for 3–5 minutes until it turns a deep golden colour, pressing gently with a spatula. Carefully turn with the spatula and cook on the second side for 2–3 minutes, or until deep golden brown all over.

Remove from the frying pan, transfer to a plate and cut in half. Let cool for a few minutes before serving. Repeat for the remaining sandwich if necessary.

NOTE Vegetarians should note that kimchi often contains fish as part of the seasoning.

WELSH RAREBIT

An exquisite vehicle for some wonderful, typical British ingredients: intense Cheddar, tangy Worcestershire sauce and mellow mustard powder, all bound together with the bitterness of ale. Incredibly simple and deeply satisfying, you can serve this anytime of day or night.

4 slices ciabatta or sourdough bread
30 g/2 tbsp unsalted butter, plus extra for spreading
30 g/3 tbsp plain/all-purpose flour
125 ml/½ cup ale, at room temperature
1 tsp mustard powder
150 g/5½ oz. mature/sharp Cheddar, grated/shredded
1 tbsp Worcestershire sauce
pinch of ground cayenne pepper

SERVES 2

Butter each of the bread slices on one side and arrange them buttered-side down on a board.

In a small saucepan over low heat, combine the butter and flour, stirring until melted. Pour the ale in gradually and stir continuously until the mixture thickens. Add the mustard powder, cheese, Worcestershire sauce and cayenne pepper, and stir to just melt the cheese before removing the pan from the heat.

Put two slices of the bread in a large frying pan/skillet, butter-side down. If you can't fit two pieces of bread in the pan, cook them one at a time. Top each slice with half of the cheese, then enclose with the other slices of bread, butter-side up.

Turn the heat to medium and cook for 3–4 minutes on the first side, then carefully turn with a large spatula and cook on the other side for 1–2 minutes more until golden brown all over.

Remove from the pan and cut in half. Let cool for a few minutes before serving.

WEEKEND QUESADILLAS

This recipe is basically cheesy loaded scrambled eggs sandwiched between two crispy wraps, what's not to like about that?

2 tbsp olive oil
100 g/3½ oz. mushrooms, thinly sliced
100 g/3½ oz. bacon lardons
50 g/2 oz. spinach
4 eggs
40 g/1½ oz. Cheddar, grated/shredded
4 tortilla wraps, 20-cm/8-inch
   diameter
salt and black pepper

SERVES 2

Add the oil to a medium or large, non-stick frying pan/skillet and set over high heat. Once hot, add the mushrooms and fry for 3 minutes, until softening and starting to colour slightly. Add the lardons to the pan and continue to fry for 3–5 minutes until the bacon is golden and the mushrooms are well browned.

Next, add the spinach and stir it through the mushroom mixture until it wilts – this should only take a minute. Scoop everything out of the pan and onto a plate, then wipe the pan clean with a paper towel (don't wash it as you're about to use it again).

Next, whisk the eggs in a bowl, season well, then add the mushroom mixture and briefly mix. The residual heat might start to cook the eggs slightly, but that's fine.

The grated cheese is used to create a barrier for the egg mix, so sprinkle the cheese in a 2.5 cm/1 inch thick ring around the edge of two of the tortillas.

Place one of these tortillas in the frying pan, spoon half the egg mixture into the centre and spread it up to the ring of cheese. Gently place a second plain tortilla on top and fry for about 2–3 minutes until the egg is starting to set and the base tortilla is crispy. Using a spatula and some confidence, flip the quesadilla over and fry on the other side for 2–3 minutes. Transfer to a board and repeat with the remaining ingredients. Slice up the quesadillas like a pizza and enjoy.

BURGER SCAMORZA

Scamorza is an Italian smoked cheese, similar to mozzarella in that it has the same beautiful melting quality, but with a little more punch.

2 white burger buns
vegetable oil, for brushing and frying
300 g/10½ oz. scamorza
    or mozzarella, sliced
tomato ketchup, to serve
gherkin/pickle spears, to serve

BURGERS
250 g/9 oz. minced/ground beef
1 small onion, grated/shredded
½ tsp garlic powder
dash of Worcestershire sauce (optional)
½ tsp salt
freshly ground black pepper

SERVES 2

Slice the burger buns in half widthways. Brush the bun halves lightly on the outside with vegetable oil. Set aside.

For the burgers, in a mixing bowl, combine the beef, onion, garlic powder, Worcestershire sauce (if using), salt and pepper and mix well. Shape into two thin patties.

Heat up some vegetable oil in a large, heavy-based non-stick frying pan/skillet over medium heat. When the pan is hot, cook the burgers for 3–5 minutes on each side, depending on how well-done you like your meat. Transfer the cooked patties to a plate and set aside.

Clean the frying pan. Place the bottoms of the burger buns, oil-side down, in the pan (without turning the heat on); you may have to cook them one at a time if they won't fit in the pan. Top each slice with one-quarter of the scamorza slices, then carefully place a patty on top. Follow this with another quarter of the cheese, so that the meat is nicely surrounded by cheese. Finally, cover with the burger bun tops, oil-side up.

Turn the heat to medium and cook the first side for 3–5 minutes until deep golden, pressing gently with a spatula. Carefully turn with a large spatula and cook on the other side, for 2–3 minutes more or until deep golden brown all over. Let cool for a few minutes before serving.

CHAPTER 2
PASTA & PIZZA

CLASSIC MAC 'N' CHEESE

This simple recipe makes a creamy macaroni and cheese that can be used as a base for further experimentation. Combining two mild cheeses, such as Cheddar and Monterey Jack, gives this dish a delicious yet delicate taste.

handful of coarse sea salt
500 g/1 lb. 2oz. macaroni
50 g/1 cup fresh breadcrumbs
salt and black pepper

BÉCHAMEL SAUCE

50 g/3½ tbsp unsalted butter
60 g/6 tbsp plain/all-purpose flour
625 ml/2½ cups milk
1 tsp fine sea salt
150 g/5½ oz. Monterey Jack or other
   mild, semi-hard cheese, grated/
   shredded
150 g/5½ oz. medium Cheddar,
   grated/shredded

SERVES 6–8

Bring a large saucepan of water to the boil. Add the coarse sea salt, then let the water return to a rolling boil. Add the macaroni, stir well and cook according to the package instructions until very tender. Stir periodically to prevent the macaroni from sticking together. When cooked, drain, rinse well under running water and let drip dry in a colander.

Preheat the grill/broiler to medium.

To make the béchamel sauce, melt the butter in a saucepan. Stir in the flour and cook, stirring continuously, for 1 minute. Pour in the milk in a steady stream, whisking continuously, and continue to whisk for 3–5 minutes until the sauce begins to thicken. Season with the fine sea salt. Remove from the heat and add the cheeses, mixing well with a spoon to incorporate. Taste and adjust the seasoning.

Put the cooked macaroni in a large mixing bowl. Pour over the hot béchamel sauce and mix well. Adjust the seasoning to taste.

Transfer the macaroni mixture to a baking dish and spread evenly. Top with a good grinding of black pepper and sprinkle the breadcrumbs evenly over the top. Grill/broil for about 5–10 minutes until the top is crunchy and golden brown, then serve immediately.

SMOKY MAC 'N' CHEESE
WITH CARAMELIZED ONION

There are many different types of smoked cheese, some of which have actually been smoked and those that simply have added smoke flavouring. This no-fuss recipe works well with either, so use whatever is readily available.

handful of coarse sea salt
500 g/1 lb. 2 oz. macaroni
3 tbsp vegetable oil
750 g/1 lb. 10 oz. onions, red and white, halved and thinly sliced
1 heaped tsp light brown sugar
3 tbsp balsamic vinegar
1 quantity Béchamel Sauce (see page 47), replacing the Monterey Jack with 200 g/7 oz. smoked cheese and reducing the quantity of Cheddar to 100 g/3½ oz.
50 g/1 cup fresh breadcrumbs
salt and black pepper

SERVES 6–8

Cook the macaroni according to the instructions on page 47.

Heat the oil in a large frying pan/skillet. Add the onions and cook over high heat for 15–20 minutes, stirring occasionally, until brown and caramelized. Add the sugar and vinegar and cook, stirring, until the mixture is almost completely dry; reduce the heat to prevent burning, if necessary. Season with salt and pepper, and set aside.

Preheat the grill/broiler to medium.

Prepare the béchamel sauce according to the instructions on page 47. Remove from the heat and add the cheeses, mixing well with a spoon to incorporate. Taste and adjust the seasoning.

Put the cooked macaroni in a large mixing bowl. Add the onions, pour over the hot béchamel sauce and mix well. Taste and adjust the seasoning. Transfer the macaroni mixture to a baking dish and spread evenly. Top with a good grinding of black pepper and sprinkle the breadcrumbs over the top.

Grill/broil for 5–10 minutes until the top is golden brown. Serve immediately.

TRUFFLED MAC 'N' CHEESE

In order to get the best results from this gourmet recipe, the key is to use the highest quality cheeses you can find. Choose a good sharp Cheddar, a Parmesan Reggiano and another strong hard cheese, such as Lincolnshire Poacher or Gruyère.

handful of coarse sea salt

500 g/1 lb. 2 oz. macaroni

1 quantity Béchamel Sauce (see page 47), replacing the Monterey Jack and Cheddar with 100 g/3½ oz. mature/sharp Cheddar, 100 g/3½ oz. Lincolnshire Poacher or Gruyère and 100 g/3½ oz. Parmesan

2 tbsp truffle paste or truffle oil

1 preserved truffle, finely chopped, reserving 3 slices to decorate

50 g/1 cup fresh breadcrumbs

salt and black pepper

SERVES 6–8

Cook the macaroni according to the instructions on page 47.

Preheat the grill/broiler to medium–hot.

Prepare the béchamel sauce according to the instructions on page 47. Remove from the heat and add the cheeses and truffle paste or truffle oil, mixing well with a spoon to incorporate. Taste and adjust the seasoning.

Put the cooked macaroni in a large mixing bowl. Stir in the chopped truffle, pour over the hot béchamel sauce and mix well. Taste and adjust the seasoning. Transfer the macaroni mixture to a baking dish and spread evenly. Top with a good grinding of black pepper and sprinkle the breadcrumbs evenly over the top. Decorate with the reserved truffle slices.

Grill/broil for 5–10 minutes until the top is crunchy and golden brown. Serve immediately.

ROASTED ASPARAGUS & PECORINO MAC 'N' CHEESE

Asparagus has such a dominant flavour that it can be difficult to find a suitable partner. However, the equally pervasive Pecorino stands up to the task beautifully.

handful of coarse sea salt
500 g/1 lb. 2 oz. macaroni
800 g/1 lb. 12 oz. asparagus, trimmed
2–3 tbsp vegetable oil
finely grated zest of 1 lemon
1 quantity Béchamel Sauce
    (see page 47), replacing the
    Monterey Jack and Cheddar with
    200 g/7 oz. Pecorino
50 g/1 cup fresh breadcrumbs
salt and black pepper

SERVES 6–8

Cook the macaroni according to the instructions on page 47.

Preheat the oven to 200°C (400°F) Gas 6.

Arrange the asparagus in a single layer on a baking sheet, sprinkle over the oil and toss to coat lightly. Roast in the preheated oven for 10–15 minutes until just charred. Remove the asparagus from the oven, cut it in half and put it in a very large bowl. Add the lemon zest, season lightly with salt and set aside.

Preheat the grill/broiler to medium.

Prepare the béchamel sauce according to the instructions on page 47. Remove from the heat and add the cheese, mixing well with a spoon to incorporate. Taste and adjust the seasoning.

Put the cooked macaroni in the bowl with the asparagus. Pour over the hot béchamel sauce and mix well. Taste and adjust the seasoning. Transfer the macaroni mixture to a baking dish and spread evenly. Top with a good grinding of black pepper and sprinkle the breadcrumbs evenly over the top.

Grill/broil for 5–10 minutes until the top is crunchy and golden brown. Serve immediately.

PROVENÇAL TOMATO & GOAT'S CHEESE MAC 'N' CHEESE

A tasty trio that sings of Mediterranean sunshine: thinly sliced goat's cheese, thyme-scented cherry tomatoes and fresh basil.

handful of coarse sea salt
500 g/1 lb. 2 oz. macaroni
500 g/1 lb. cherry tomatoes, halved
small head of garlic, cloves separated
　but skins left on
few sprigs of fresh thyme, chopped
2–3 tbsp extra-virgin olive oil
600 ml/2½ cups double/heavy cream
leaves from a small bunch of fresh
　basil, thinly sliced
100 g/3½ oz. hard goat's cheese,
　grated/shredded
2 x 60-g/2-oz. Crottin de Chavignol
　or other mild goat's cheese,
　ends trimmed, sliced
50 g/1 cup fresh breadcrumbs
salt and black pepper

SERVES 6–8

Cook the macaroni according to the instructions on page 47.

Preheat the oven to 190°C (375°F) Gas 5.

Arrange the halved tomatoes and garlic in a single layer on a baking sheet; some skin-side up and some not. Sprinkle over the thyme and oil and toss to coat lightly. Roast in the oven for 15–20 minutes until just charred. Slip the garlic cloves out of their skins and chop finely. Set aside. Transfer the tomatoes to a very large bowl and season lightly with salt. Set aside.

Preheat the grill/broiler to medium–hot.

Put the cream in a large saucepan and bring just to the boil, stirring. Add the basil, chopped garlic and a pinch of salt, then reduce the heat. Add the grated goat's cheese and stir to melt.

Put the cooked macaroni in the bowl with the tomatoes. Pour over the hot cream sauce and mix well. Taste and adjust the seasoning. Transfer the macaroni mixture to a baking dish and spread evenly. Top with a good grinding of black pepper and arrange the Crottin de Chavignol slices on top of the macaroni.

Sprinkle with the breadcrumbs and grill/broil for 5–10 minutes until the top is crunchy and golden brown. Serve immediately.

AUBERGINE PARMIGIANA MAC 'N' CHEESE

Dripping in melted cheese, this is a real a crowd pleaser.

handful of coarse sea salt

500 g/1 lb. 2 oz. macaroni

4–5 tbsp vegetable oil

1 large onion, finely chopped

1 tsp dried thyme

1 tsp dried oregano

1 tsp dried rosemary

3 garlic cloves, finely chopped

400-g/14-oz. can chopped tomatoes

1 aubergine/eggplant, sliced

1 quantity Béchamel Sauce
(see page 47), replacing the
Monterey Jack and Cheddar
with 100 g/3½ oz. Fontina and
100 g/3½ oz. Parmesan

125 g/4 oz. grated/shredded
mozzarella

leaves from 2–3 sprigs fresh basil,
coarsely torn

50 g/1 cup fresh breadcrumbs

salt and black pepper

SERVES 6–8

Cook the macaroni according to the instructions on page 47.

Preheat the oven to 200°C (400°F) Gas 6.

Heat 2 tablespoons of the oil in a large lidded sauté pan. Add the onion and cook over medium heat for 5 minutes until just golden. Add the herbs and garlic and cook gently for 1 minute (don't let the garlic burn). Add the tomatoes and a teaspoon of salt, and simmer gently for 20–30 minutes until very thick.

Meanwhile, arrange the aubergine slices in a single layer on a baking sheet and sprinkle over the remaining oil. Roast in the preheated oven for 15–20 minutes until tender and just charred. Remove, season lightly with salt and add to the tomatoes. Simmer gently while you prepare the béchamel sauce.

Preheat the grill/broiler to medium.

Prepare the béchamel sauce according to the instructions on page 47. Remove from the heat and add the Fontina and Parmesan, mixing well. Taste and adjust the seasoning.

Put the cooked macaroni in a large mixing bowl. Stir in the aubergine mixture and hot béchamel sauce. Transfer the macaroni mixture to a baking dish and spread evenly. Top with the mozzarella, basil leaves and a good grinding of black pepper and sprinkle the breadcrumbs evenly over the top.

Grill/broil for 5–10 minutes until the top is crunchy and golden brown. Serve immediately.

2 tbsp olive oil

1 onion, halved and sliced

225 g/8 oz. frozen mixed grilled sweet peppers, or 1 red and 1 yellow (bell) pepper, deseeded and sliced

3 garlic cloves, crushed

1 tsp dried thyme

¼–½ tsp dried chilli/hot red pepper flakes

2 x 400-g/14-oz. cans chopped tomatoes

pinch of sugar

large handful of fresh basil or flat-leaf parsley leaves, chopped

500 g/1 lb. 2 oz. small filled ravioli or cappeletti

75 g/2½ oz. Gruyère or medium Cheddar, grated/shredded

2 tbsp grated/shredded Parmesan

salt and black pepper

SERVES 4–6

CHEESY RAVIOLI BAKE
WITH GRILLED SWEET PEPPERS

Fresh or dried ravioli both work well here, and any filling will do, but goat's cheese and pesto is an especially good one. Frozen mixed grilled sweet peppers are fantastic for stirring into anything that needs a quick lift but if you cannot find any, simply thinly slice a red and a yellow pepper and sweat them with the onions.

Preheat the oven to 200°C (400°F) Gas 6.

Heat the oil in a large saucepan. Add the onion and cook over low heat for 3–5 minutes until soft. Add the peppers, garlic, thyme and chilli flakes, and cook, stirring, for 2–3 minutes.

Stir in the tomatoes and sugar, season and simmer, uncovered, for 15 minutes. Taste and adjust the seasoning if necessary. Stir in the basil.

Cook the ravioli according to the package instructions and drain well.

Tip the cooked ravioli into the sauce and stir gently to coat. Transfer to a lightly greased baking dish, spread evenly and sprinkle both the cheeses over the top.

Bake in the preheated oven for 20–30 minutes until the cheese is melted and golden. Serve immediately.

SPICY CORN MAC 'N' CHEESE

The best part of this is the way the crunchy sweetness of the fresh corn kernels is complemented by the smoky toasted cumin. Don't be tempted to use frozen or canned corn in this recipe, as it simply will not taste the same.

handful of coarse sea salt

500 g/1 lb. 2 oz. macaroni

4 corn cobs

1½ tsp cumin seeds

1 quantity Béchamel Sauce
    (see page 47), increasing the
    quantities of Monterey Jack and
    Cheddar to 200 g/7 oz. each

1 red chilli/chile, finely chopped
    and deseeded, if liked

1 green chilli/chile, finely chopped
    and deseeded, if liked

few sprigs of fresh coriander/cilantro,
    finely chopped

50 g/1 cup fresh breadcrumbs

salt and black pepper

SERVES 6–8

Cook the macaroni according to the instructions on page 47.

Bring a large saucepan of water to the boil. Add the corn cobs and cook for 3 minutes. Drain and let cool slightly, then scrape off the kernels with a sharp knife and set aside.

Heat a small frying pan/skillet until hot but not smoking. Add the cumin seeds and cook until aromatic and beginning to brown. Transfer to a dish to cool, then grind to a powder with a mortar and pestle and set aside.

Preheat the grill/broiler to medium.

Prepare the béchamel sauce according to the instructions on page 47. Remove from the heat and add the cheeses, chillies and cumin, mixing well. Taste and adjust the seasoning.

Put the cooked macaroni in a large mixing bowl. Add the corn and coriander, pour over the hot béchamel sauce and mix well. Taste and adjust the seasoning. Transfer the macaroni mixture to a baking dish and spread evenly. Top with a good grinding of black pepper and sprinkle the breadcrumbs evenly over the top.

Grill/broil for 5–10 minutes until the top is crunchy and golden brown. Serve immediately.

SMOKED HADDOCK & SPINACH MAC 'N' CHEESE

Cheddar, smoked haddock and wilted spinach are a classic combination.

handful of coarse sea salt
500 g/1 lb. 2 oz. macaroni
600 g/1¼ lbs. smoked haddock fillets
2 tbsp vegetable oil
500 g/1 lb. 2 oz. fresh spinach
15 g/1 tbsp unsalted butter
1 large shallot, finely chopped
600 ml/2½ cups double/heavy cream
pinch of grated nutmeg
200 g/7 oz. medium Cheddar,
    grated/shredded
50 g/1 cup fresh breadcrumbs
salt and black pepper

SERVES 6–8

Cook the macaroni according to the instructions on page 47.

Arrange the haddock fillets in a microwaveable dish in a single layer, skin-side down, and add just enough water to cover. Cover with clingfilm/plastic wrap and microwave on high for 4–5 minutes, or until the flesh flakes easily. Flake the fish, discard the skin and cooking liquid and remove any bones. Set aside.

Heat 1 tablespoon of the oil in a deep frying pan/skillet. Add half the spinach and cook over high heat, stirring, until wilted. Season with salt and pepper, then transfer to a chopping board and spread out to cool. Repeat for the remaining spinach. Chop all the spinach coarsely and transfer to a large mixing bowl.

Preheat the grill/broiler to medium–hot.

In the same frying pan, heat the butter and remaining oil. Add the shallot and cook over high heat for 2–3 minutes until just golden, stirring occasionally. Add the cream, nutmeg and a good pinch of salt, bring just to the boil, then reduce the heat.

Add the haddock and cheese to the spinach and pour over the hot cream mixture. Stir well to melt the cheese, then add the macaroni and mix well. Taste and adjust the seasoning. Transfer to a baking dish and spread evenly. Top with a good grinding of black pepper and sprinkle the breadcrumbs over the top.

Grill/broil for 5–10 minutes until the top is crunchy and golden brown. Serve immediately.

3 tbsp olive oil
1 small onion, finely chopped
1 carrot, finely chopped
2–3 celery sticks, from the inner
    section, with leaves, finely chopped
1 red, yellow or orange (bell) pepper,
    deseeded and finely chopped
100 g/1½ cups diced mushrooms
3 garlic cloves, finely chopped
125 ml/½ cup dry white or red wine
½–1 tsp dried chilli/hot red pepper
    flakes
½ tbsp fresh thyme leaves
    or 1 tsp dried thyme
large handful of fresh parsley
    or basil leaves, finely chopped
400-g/14-oz. can chopped tomatoes
700 ml/3 cups passata/
    strained tomatoes
pinch of sugar
500 g/1 lb. 2 oz. dried rigatoni
500 g/1 lb. 2 oz. mozzarella, sliced
salt and black pepper

SERVES 4–6

BAKED RIGATONI
WITH MOZZARELLA

Putting the mozzarella in the middle as well as on top of this pasta bake means you get a lovely inner layer of melting cheese, as well as a browned topping. Blissfully simple to make. Other vegetables can be used here according to what's in season or to hand – sweetcorn, broccoli and spinach will all work nicely here.

Heat the oil in a large saucepan, add the onion and cook over low heat for 3–5 minutes until soft. Add the carrot, celery and pepper. Season and cook for 2–3 minutes. Stir in the mushrooms and garlic, and cook for 1 minute more. Add the wine and cook for 1 minute more. Stir in the chilli flakes, thyme, parsley, tomatoes, passata and sugar. Season generously and stir. Reduce the heat and simmer, uncovered, for 20–30 minutes. Taste and adjust the seasoning if necessary.

Meanwhile, cook the pasta according to the package instructions until al dente. Drain well and set aside.

Preheat the oven to 200°C (400°F) Gas 6.

Combine the cooked pasta and the vegetable sauce and mix well. Spread half the pasta in the prepared dish evenly. Top with half of the mozzarella. Top with the remaining pasta in an even layer and arrange the remaining mozzarella slices on top.

Bake in the preheated oven for 25–30 minutes until the cheese melts and bubbles. Serve immediately.

MUSHROOM, TARRAGON & TALEGGIO PASTA BAKE

It is the strong aroma and fruity tang of taleggio in this recipe that transforms it from an ordinary mushroom and cheese dish into something truly sublime. Use fresh tarragon if you can find it.

handful of coarse sea salt

500 g/1 lb. 2 oz. short pasta

300 g/10 oz. Portobello mushrooms, stems trimmed level with cap

2–3 tbsp vegetable oil

leaves from a few sprigs of fresh parsley, finely chopped

leaves from a few sprigs of fresh tarragon, finely chopped

600 ml/2½ cups double/heavy cream

100 g/3½ oz. Cheddar, grated/shredded

50 g/1¾ oz. Parmesan, grated/shredded

250 g/9 oz. Taleggio, thinly sliced

salt and black pepper

SERVES 6–8

Cook the pasta according to the instructions on page 47.

Preheat the oven to 200°C (400°F) Gas 6.

Arrange the mushrooms in a single layer on a baking sheet, stems up, and brush with the oil. Season lightly with salt, sprinkle over the herbs and roast in the preheated oven for 15–20 minutes until tender. Let cool slightly. Slice the mushrooms and set aside.

Preheat the grill/broiler to medium.

Put the cream in a large saucepan and bring just to the boil, stirring occasionally, then reduce the heat. Add the Cheddar and Parmesan and half the Taleggio, stir well to melt, then taste and adjust the seasoning.

Put the cooked pasta in a large mixing bowl. Stir in half the sliced mushrooms, pour over the hot cream sauce and mix well. Taste and adjust the seasoning. Transfer the pasta mixture to a baking dish and spread evenly. Top with the remaining mushrooms and Taleggio slices and a good grinding of black pepper.

Grill/broil for 5–10 minutes until the top is golden and serve immediately.

REBLOCHON, LEEK & BACON PASTA BAKE

This delicious French-inspired mac 'n' cheese combines the traditional ingredients of the classic Alpine dish tartiflette. It's a hearty and elegant dish, making it perfect for entertaining.

handful of coarse sea salt
500 g/1 lb. 2 oz. short pasta
3 large leeks (about 500 g/1 lb. 2 oz.), sliced into rounds
3 tbsp vegetable oil
200 g/7 oz. bacon lardons
300 ml/1¼ cups double/heavy cream
300 g/1¼ cups crème fraîche or sour cream
100 g/3½ oz. mild Cheddar or Monterey Jack, grated/shredded
250 g/9 oz. Reblochon or other rich, soft cow's milk cheese such as Brie, half finely diced and half thinly sliced
50 g/1 cup fresh breadcrumbs
salt and black pepper

SERVES 6–8

Cook the pasta according to the instructions on page 47.

Preheat the oven to 180°C (350°F) Gas 4.

Arrange the leeks in a single layer on a baking sheet. Sprinkle over 2 tablespoons of the oil and toss to coat lightly. Roast in the preheated oven for about 15 minutes until tender and just charred. Transfer the leeks to a very large bowl. Season lightly with salt and set aside.

Heat the remaining oil in a sauté pan. Add the bacon and cook over medium–high heat for 5–10 minutes until well browned. Drain away the excess fat and add the bacon to the leeks.

Preheat the grill/broiler to medium–hot.

Combine the cream and crème fraîche in a large saucepan and bring just to the boil, stirring. Remove from the heat, add the grated cheese and diced Reblochon and stir to melt.

Put the pasta in the bowl with the leeks and bacon. Add the hot cream sauce and mix well. Taste and adjust the seasoning. Transfer the mixture to a baking dish and spread evenly. Arrange the Reblochon slices on top, add a good grinding of black pepper and sprinkle the breadcrumbs over the top.

Grill/broil for 5–10 minutes until the top is crunchy and golden brown. Serve immediately.

PASTA BAKE WITH HOT DOGS, CHEESE, ONIONS & MUSTARD

For best results, be sure to use both good-quality frankfurters and strong tasting cheese. Red Leicester works well here, both for its tangy taste and orange hue. If unavailable, a strong Cheddar used in combination with a milder orange-coloured hard cheese will also work.

handful of coarse sea salt
500 g/1 lb. 2 oz. short pasta
2 tbsp vegetable oil
1 large onion, coarsely chopped
350–400 g/12–14 oz. frankfurters/
    hot dogs (about 8–10), sliced into
    bite-size pieces
1 quantity Béchamel Sauce
    (see page 47), replacing the
    Monterey Jack and Cheddar with
    300 g/10½ oz. Red Leicester
2 heaped tbsp wholegrain mustard
50 g/1 cup fresh breadcrumbs
salt and black pepper

SERVES 6–8

Cook the pasta according to the instructions on page 47.

Heat the oil in a large frying pan/skillet. Add the onion and cook over high heat for 5–8 minutes until brown and caramelized, stirring occasionally. Season lightly with salt and pepper. Add the frankfurter pieces and cook for 2–3 minutes until just browned. Set aside.

Prepare the béchamel sauce according to the instructions on page 47. Remove from the heat and add the cheeses and the mustard, mixing well. Taste and adjust the seasoning.

Preheat the grill/broiler to medium–hot.

Put the cooked pasta in a large mixing bowl. Pour over the hot béchamel sauce, stir in the frankfurter mixture and mix well. Taste and adjust the seasoning. Transfer the macaroni mixture to a baking dish and spread evenly. Top with a grinding of black pepper and sprinkle the breadcrumbs evenly over the top.

Grill/broil for 5–10 minutes until the top is crunchy and golden brown. Serve immediately.

BBQ CHICKEN MAC 'N' CHEESE

Ideal for hectic households, this straightforward combination has tastes that appeal to all generations, with the added bonus of being very quick to prepare. Serve with corn, coleslaw and a green salad.

handful of coarse sea salt
500 g/1 lb. 2 oz. macaroni
250 g/9 oz. skinless and boneless poached or roasted chicken, shredded
250 ml/1 cup barbecue sauce
1 quantity Béchamel Sauce (see page 47), omitting the Monterey Jack and increasing the quantity of Cheddar to 200 g/7 oz.
250 g/9 oz. mozzarella, half shredded and half sliced
50 g/1 cup fresh breadcrumbs
salt and black pepper

SERVES 6–8

Cook the macaroni according to the instructions on page 47.

Put the shredded chicken and the barbecue sauce in a large bowl and mix well. Taste and adjust the seasoning. Set aside.

Preheat the grill/broiler to medium.

Prepare the béchamel sauce according to the instructions on page 47. Remove from the heat and add the Cheddar and shredded mozzarella, mixing well with a spoon to incorporate. Taste and adjust the seasoning.

Put the cooked macaroni in a large mixing bowl. Pour over the hot béchamel sauce, add the chicken mixture and mix well. Taste and adjust the seasoning.

Transfer the macaroni to a baking dish and spread evenly. Top with the sliced mozzarella and a good grinding of black pepper and sprinkle the breadcrumbs evenly over the top.

Grill/broil for 5–10 minutes until the top is crunchy and golden brown. Serve immediately.

PANCETTA, GORGONZOLA & TOMATO MAC 'N' CHEESE

A strongly tasting cheese such as Gorgonzola pairs beautifully with a creamy sauce here. Smoky pancetta and a tomato reduction are both equally punchy and match up to the pungent cheese well.

handful of coarse sea salt
500 g/1 lb. 2 oz. macaroni
2 tbsp olive oil
1 onion, finely chopped
200 g/7 oz. pancetta, chopped
½ tsp dried thyme
400-g/14-oz. can chopped tomatoes
pinch of sugar
600 ml/2½ cups double/heavy cream
200 g/7 oz. Gorgonzola, crumbled
50 g/1¾ oz. Parmesan, grated/
   shredded
50 g/1 cup fresh breadcrumbs
salt and black pepper

SERVES 6–8

Cook the macaroni according to the instructions on page 47.

Heat the oil in a large frying pan/skillet. Add the onion and cook over high heat for about 5 minutes until just caramelized, stirring occasionally. Stir in the pancetta and thyme, and cook for 2–3 minutes until browned, stirring occasionally. Add the tomatoes, sugar and 1 teaspoon salt and simmer very gently for 15–30 minutes until the mixture has reduced to a jam-like consistency. Transfer to a large bowl and set aside.

Preheat the grill/broiler to medium–hot.

Put the cream in a large saucepan and bring just to the boil, then reduce the heat. Add the cheeses and stir well to melt.

Put the cooked macaroni in the bowl with the tomato mixture. Pour over the hot cream sauce and mix well. Taste and adjust the seasoning. Transfer the macaroni mixture to a baking dish and spread out evenly. Top with a good grinding of black pepper and sprinkle the breadcrumbs evenly over the top.

Grill/broil for about 5–10 minutes until the top is crunchy and golden brown. Serve immediately.

HAM HOCK & SMOKED MOZZARELLA PASTA BAKE

This sophisticated take on the classic combination of ham, cheese and pasta uses smoked mozzarella, which was made to be melted.

handful of coarse sea salt

500 g/1 lb. 2 oz. pasta

190 g/6½ oz. cooked ham hock, shredded

250 g/9 oz. smoked mozzarella, thinly sliced

1 quantity Béchamel Sauce (see page 47), omitting the Monterey Jack and reducing the quantity of Cheddar to 100 g/3½ oz.

50 g/1 cup fresh breadcrumbs

salt and black pepper

SERVES 6–8

Cook the pasta according to the instructions on page 47.

Combine the ham hock and half the mozzarella and mix well. Taste and adjust the seasoning. Set aside.

Preheat the grill/broiler to medium.

Prepare the béchamel sauce according to the instructions on page 47. Remove from the heat and add the cheese, mixing well to incorporate. Taste and adjust the seasoning.

Put the cooked pasta in a large mixing bowl. Pour over the hot béchamel sauce and the ham mixture and mix well. Taste and adjust the seasoning. Transfer the mixture to a baking dish and spread evenly. Top with the remaining mozzarella and a good grinding of black pepper and sprinkle the breadcrumbs evenly over the top.

Grill/broil for 5–10 minutes until the top is crunchy and golden brown. Serve immediately.

SERRANO HAM, SMOKED PAPRIKA & SPANISH BLUE MAC 'N' CHEESE

This trio of ingredients has long been popular in Spanish cooking, and this pasta dish is yet another excuse for bringing them together. A robust and comforting dish that brings the warmth of the Mediterranean to the kitchen, this recipe is perfect for brightening up cold winter days.

handful of coarse sea salt

500 g/1 lb. 2 oz. macaroni

2–3 tbsp vegetable oil

1 onion, finely chopped

1 red (bell) pepper, sliced

2 tsp sweet smoked paprika

100 g/3½ oz. Serrano or other cured ham, finely chopped

1 garlic clove, finely chopped

400-g/14-oz. can chopped tomatoes

60 ml/¼ cup red wine

600 ml/2½ cups double/heavy cream

200 g/7 oz. mild Cheddar cheese or Monterey Jack, grated/shredded

100 g/3½ oz. Spanish blue cheese, crumbled

50 g/1 cup fresh breadcrumbs

salt and black pepper

SERVES 6–8

Cook the macaroni according to the instructions on page 47.

Heat the oil in a large sauté pan with a lid over medium–high heat. Add the onion and red pepper, and cook for about 5 minutes until the onion is just golden. Stir in the paprika, ham and garlic, and cook gently for 1 minute, taking care not to let the garlic burn. Add the tomatoes and wine, and simmer very gently for 15–30 minutes until the mixture has reduced to a jam-like consistency. Taste and adjust the seasoning.

Preheat the grill/broiler to medium–hot.

Put the cream in a large saucepan and bring just to the boil, then reduce the heat. Add the cheeses and stir well to melt.

Put the cooked macaroni in a large bowl. Pour over the hot cream sauce, add the ham mixture and mix well. Taste and adjust the seasoning. Transfer the macaroni mixture to a baking dish and spread evenly. Top with a good grinding of black pepper and sprinkle the breadcrumbs evenly over the top.

Grill/broil for 5–10 minutes until the top is crunchy and golden brown. Serve immediately.

PIZZA BIANCA

Neapolitans naturally call pizza without tomatoes pizza bianca. All the focus will be on the mozzarella, so this has to be the finest buffalo mozzarella. This cheese tends to be quite wet, so squeeze out any watery whey before slicing it.

1 quantity Pizza Dough (see page 77)
200 g/7 oz. buffalo mozzarella or
    cow's milk mozzarella (fior di latte)
handful of small fresh sage leaves
extra-virgin olive oil, to drizzle
salt and black pepper
semolina, for dusting
2 large baking sheets, lightly oiled

MAKES 2

Prepare the dough according to the instructions on page 77.

Preheat the oven to 250°C (475°F) Gas 9 and sprinkle the prepared baking sheets with semolina.

Lightly squeeze any excess moisture out of the mozzarella, then slice it and leave the slices on paper towels for 5 minutes to absorb any remaining moisture.

Tip the dough out of the bowl and press down on it to knock out the air. Divide it in half. Pull and shape one piece of dough into a large circle, then place it on a prepared baking sheet and push it out towards the edges. (It doesn't have to be a perfect circle!) Arrange half the mozzarella evenly over the pizza crust, leaving a 1-cm/½-inch rim around the edge. Repeat with the other piece of dough and the remaining cheese. Scatter the sage over the cheese, then season and drizzle with oil.

Bake in the preheated oven for 8–10 minutes until the dough has puffed up and the cheese is brown and bubbling. Remove from the oven and sprinkle with freshly ground black pepper. Serve immediately.

ITALIAN FOUR-CHEESE PIZZA

Try making the classic 'quattro formaggi' with top-quality Italian cheeses. The homemade version is far superior than versions of this that come ready-made.

400 ml/1⅔ cups passata/strained
    tomatoes
140 g/5 oz. Pecorino Toscano
    (rind removed), sliced
140 g/5 oz. Taleggio (rind removed)
    or buffalo mozzarella, sliced
85 g/3 oz. Gorgonzola piccante,
    crumbled
25 g/¾ oz. Parmesan, grated/
    shredded
handful of fresh oregano or basil leaves
freshly ground black pepper

PIZZA DOUGH
175 g/1¼ cups strong white bread flour
130 g/1 cup cake flour
1 tsp fine sea salt
1 envelope fast-action dried yeast
½ tsp sugar
2 tbsp olive oil, plus extra to drizzle
about 175 ml/¾ cup hand-hot water
semolina, for dusting
2 large baking sheets, lightly oiled

MAKES 2 PIZZAS

To make the pizza dough, sift the flours into a bowl with the salt, yeast and sugar. Mix together, then form a hollow in the centre. Add the olive oil and half the hand-hot water, and stir to incorporate the flour. Gradually add as much of the remaining water as you need to pull the dough together. (It should take most of it – you need a slightly wet dough.) Turn the dough out and knead for 10 minutes until smooth and elastic (use a little extra flour to prevent the dough sticking if necessary). Put the dough into a lightly oiled bowl, cover with plastic wrap, and leave in a warm place until doubled in size; 1–1¼ hours.

Preheat the oven to 250°C (475°F) Gas 9 and sprinkle the prepared baking sheets with semolina.

Tip the dough out of the bowl and press down on it to knock out the air. Divide it in half. Pull and shape one piece of dough into a large circle, then place it on a prepared baking sheet and push it out towards the edges. (It doesn't have to be a perfect circle!) Spread half the passata over the top, then arrange half the cheeses over the top. Season with pepper. Repeat with the other piece of dough and the remaining cheese. Drizzle a little olive oil over the top of each pizza.

Bake in the preheated oven for 8–10 minutes until the dough has puffed up and the cheese is brown and bubbling. Garnish with oregano leaves and drizzle over a little more oil.

DEEP-DISH MEATBALL PIZZA PIE

Chicago-style pizza has tall sides that contain an oozy filling.

450 g/1 lb. beef meatballs
300 g/10½ oz. fresh mozzarella,
   patted dry
3 tbsp grated/shredded Parmesan

PIZZA DOUGH

¼ tbsp fast-action dried yeast
¼ tbsp sugar
60 g/¼ cup clarified butter or shortening
260 g/2 cups plain/all-purpose flour
salt

TOMATO SAUCE

1 onion, finely chopped
2 tbsp olive oil
2 garlic cloves, thinly sliced
400-g/14-oz. can tomatoes
1 pear, peeled, cored and
   chopped into small pieces
1 heaped tsp dried oregano
1 bay leaf
non-stick 20-cm/8-inch
   loose-bottomed cake pan

SERVES 4

For the dough, mix 175 ml/¾ cup water with the yeast and sugar, and leave for 5 minutes. Put the yeast mixture, butter or shortening, 130 g/1 cup flour and a pinch of salt in an electric mixer with a dough hook and mix for 5 minutes. Add 100 g/¾ cup more flour and mix until a dough forms. Add the remaining flour if needed. The dough should be wet, but shouldn't stick to your hands. Put the dough in a covered bowl in the fridge to rise overnight. Remove 2–3 hours before use.

To make the sauce, lightly sauté the onion in a heavy-based casserole dish with the olive oil and garlic. When the onion is translucent and soft, add the tomatoes, pear pieces, oregano and bay leaf. Cook slowly for 1 hour, stirring occasionally, until the pear has dissolved into the tomatoes. Remove the bay leaf and blitz the sauce with a stick blender until smooth.

Preheat the oven to its highest setting. Brown the meatballs in a frying pan/skillet and add to the tomato sauce. Pat the dough into the base of the cake pan, up the sides and firmly all around the edge using your knuckles.

Place three-quarters of the mozzarella in the bottom of the pan. Cover with the meatballs and tomato sauce. Top with the remaining mozzarella and the Parmesan. Bake in the preheated oven for 25–30 minutes until the crust is puffed and golden. If the inside is still soupy, return to the oven for 5–10 minutes.

To serve, remove the sides of the cake pan and cut into quarters with a large knife or cake server.

CHAPTER 3
GRATINS & OVEN BAKES

SWISS CHARD & GRUYÈRE GRATIN

This gratin has it all – deliciously decadent cream and melted cheese, as well as nutritious, iron-rich Swiss chard. You can add a little bacon if you want a meaty hit alongside.

800 g/1¾ lb. Swiss chard
50 g/3½ tbsp unsalted butter
75 g/½ cup plus 1 tbsp plain/
   all-purpose flour
200 ml/scant 1 cup crème fraîche
   or sour cream
300 ml/1¼ cups double/heavy cream
pinch of grated nutmeg
50 g/1 cup fresh breadcrumbs
finely grated zest of 1 lemon
   and a good squeeze of juice
50 g/3¾ oz. Gruyère, grated/shredded
1 tbsp olive oil
salt and black pepper

SERVES 6

Bring a pan of water to the boil and blanch the chard for 2–3 minutes, then drain and refresh under cold running water. Squeeze out as much of the water as possible and set aside.

Melt the butter in a pan, add the flour and cook for about 1–2 minutes. Add the crème fraîche, cream and nutmeg. Simmer for 2–3 minutes, then season to taste.

Preheat the grill/broiler to medium.

Mix the chard and the sauce together and spoon into a large ovenproof dish. Mix the breadcrumbs with the lemon zest, cheese and olive oil, and sprinkle over the top.

Put under the grill/broiler for a couple of minutes until the gratin is golden brown and bubbling. (If you like, you can mix the sauce with the chard in advance and leave until ready to cook. Heat through in a medium oven for 5–10 minutes before browning under the grill/broiler.)

Serve with a squeeze of lemon juice.

1 kg/2 lb. 4 oz. large waxy potatoes, unpeeled
knob/pat of unsalted butter
200 g/7 oz. smoked bacon lardons
1 garlic clove, thinly sliced
75 ml/scant ⅓ cup dry white wine
200 ml/scant 1 cup double/ heavy cream
300 g/11 oz. Reblochon cheese, thickly sliced
salt and black pepper

SERVES 6

TARTIFLETTE

Tartiflette is one of the most iconic melted cheese recipes from the Alps. Reblochon cheese smothers firm, waxy potatoes, making this a bubbling dish of heaven. Traditionalists would insist that it contains just cheese, potatoes and bacon, but the addition of a good glug of cream loosens the dish and gives it extra-creamy depth.

Preheat the oven to 190°C (375°F) Gas 5.

Cook the potatoes in a pan of boiling salted water for 10–12 minutes until just tender. Drain, thickly slice and set aside.

Heat the butter in a frying pan/skillet and fry the lardons until starting to crisp. Add the garlic and wine, and bubble until the wine is almost gone.

Season, remove from the heat and stir through the cream and potato slices.

Layer the potato mixture with most of the cheese slices in a large ovenproof dish, pouring over any remaining cream from the pan at the end, before topping with a final layer of cheese.

Bake in the preheated oven for 25–30 minutes until the tartiflette is golden and bubbling.

GRATIN DE CHOU-FLEUR

This is a sublimely indulgent and comforting dish, as cauliflower is a perfect partner for melted cheese.

½ cauliflower, cut into florets

2 courgettes/zucchini, thinly sliced on an angle

100 g/3½ oz. Brussels sprouts, thinly sliced

70 g/5 tbsp unsalted butter

40 g/5 tbsp plain/all-purpose flour

1 litre/quart full-fat/whole milk

200 g/7 oz. Gruyère, grated/shredded

1 tsp freshly chopped thyme

½ tsp grated nutmeg

50 g/⅔ cup dried breadcrumbs

salt and black pepper

SERVES 6

Preheat the oven to 190°C (375°F) Gas 5.

Steam the cauliflower in a large pan of boiling water fitted with a steamer basket for 5–7 minutes until the florets are just tender. Rinse them in cold water, drain and arrange them in a single layer in a buttered baking dish. Add the raw sliced courgettes and sprouts.

In a large pan over medium heat, melt the butter and whisk in the flour until it forms a smooth paste. Continue whisking and cook for about 2 minutes, then gradually add the milk, a little at a time. Add half the cheese and stir until melted. Continue whisking and cook until the sauce is heated through, smooth and thickened. Remove from the heat and season with salt, then add the thyme and nutmeg.

Pour the béchamel sauce over the cauliflower, courgettes and sprouts, and gently toss the florets to make sure they are thoroughly coated with the sauce. Bake the gratin, uncovered, in the preheated oven for 15 minutes.

Mix the remaining grated Gruyère with the breadcrumbs, and sprinkle them over the gratin.

Bake it for an additional 10–15 minutes until the gratin is hot and bubbly and the cheese is melted and browned. Sprinkle the surface of the baked gratin with black pepper and serve hot.

MUSHROOM, FONTINA, SPINACH & POTATO BAKE

Fontina is a dense, nutty Italian cheese that melts beautifully and gives the mashed potatoes a delicious golden crust. It is hearty, comforting and tasty, and will satisfy the hungriest of guests.

1 kg/2 lb. 4 oz. floury potatoes, peeled and roughly chopped
125 ml/½ cup full-fat/whole milk
pinch of grated nutmeg
125 g/9 tbsp unsalted butter, cut into cubes
500 g/1 lb. 2 oz. small chestnut mushrooms, left whole and stalks removed
4 garlic cloves, roughly chopped
4 spring onions/scallions, cut into 2-cm/¾-inch lengths
1 kg/2 lb. 4 oz. spinach, well washed and roughly chopped
200 g/7 oz. Fontina, cubed
salt and black pepper

SERVES 4–6

Put the potatoes in a large pan of lightly salted boiling water and boil for about 12–15 minutes until tender but not falling apart. Drain well, return to the warm pan and roughly mash. Add the milk and nutmeg, and season to taste with salt and pepper. Beat with a large wooden spoon or hand-held electric whisk until smooth. Stir through half of the butter. Spoon about one-third of the mixture into a baking dish.

Preheat the oven to 180°C (350°F) Gas 4.

Heat half of the remaining butter in a large frying pan/skillet set over medium heat. Add the mushrooms, garlic and spring onions, and gently fry for about 10 minutes until golden. Spoon over the potato mixture in the baking dish.

Heat the remaining butter in the frying pan and cook the spinach for 5 minutes, stirring often, until just wilted and tender. Season to taste and spoon over the mushrooms in the baking dish.

Spoon the remaining mashed potatoes on top of the spinach and scatter over the Fontina. Bake in the preheated oven for about 30 minutes until the cheese is bubbly and golden.

CHICORY GRATIN WITH HAM & BLUE CHEESE

This is a French recipe that traditionally calls for Gruyère cheese only, but the blue cheese used here makes it even better. There are many kinds of blue cheese and any one will do for this dish. You can also experiment with different kinds of ham; cured ham works especially well. Or, omit the ham altogether for an indulgent vegetarian supper.

6 chicory (about 90 g/3 oz. each), rinsed and dried

1–2 tbsp olive oil

1 quantity Béchamel Sauce (see page 47), replacing the Monterey Jack with 100 g/3½ oz. grated/shredded Gruyère and 65 g/2 oz. crumbled firm blue cheese

12 slices smoked ham

2–3 tbsp grated/shredded Gruyère or Parmesan

salt

SERVES 2

Preheat the oven to 200°C (400°F) Gas 6.

Halve the chicory lengthways. Drizzle with the oil and rub with your hands to coat evenly. Arrange in a single layer on a baking sheet. Sprinkle lightly with salt and drizzle over about 4 tablespoons water. Roast in the preheated oven for about 15 minutes until just tender when pierced with a knife. Remove from the oven and let cool. Leave the oven on.

Prepare the béchamel sauce according to the instructions on page 47. Remove from the heat and add the cheeses, mixing well with a spoon to incorporate. Taste and adjust the seasoning if needed.

When the chicory are cool enough to handle, carefully wrap each one with a slice of ham and arrange them side-by-side, seam-side down, in a baking dish. Pour over the béchamel, spreading evenly to coat. Sprinkle with the grated cheese.

Bake in the oven for 20–30 minutes until browned and bubbling. Serve immediately.

ROOT VEGETABLE GRATIN

This is a rustic hearty dish, and the melted cheese with which it is topped makes it comforting and satisfying in addition to the nourishment you get from the many different types of vegetables. It is simple to prepare too, the most time-consuming part is chopping the vegetables!

3 small turnips (about 375 g/13 oz.), peeled, halved and very thinly sliced

½ celeriac (about 325 g/11 oz.), peeled, halved and very thinly sliced

½ swede (about 450 g/1 lb.), peeled, halved and very thinly sliced

650 g/1 lb. 7 oz. waxy potatoes, peeled, halved and very thinly sliced

225 ml/scant 1 cup double/ heavy cream

100 g/⅓ cup crème fraîche or sour cream

250 ml/1 cup full-fat/whole milk

125 g/4 oz. Gruyère or medium Cheddar, grated/shredded

salt and black pepper

SERVES 4–6

Preheat the oven to 200°C (400°F) Gas 6.

Put all the vegetable slices in a large bowl and toss gently to combine. Set aside.

Combine the cream, crème fraîche and milk in a small pan and heat just to melt the crème fraîche. Stir well and season with salt and pepper.

Arrange half of the vegetables slices in a buttered baking dish. Sprinkle with a little salt and one-third of the cheese. Pour over one-third of the cream mixture.

Top with the rest of the vegetables, the remaining cheese and a sprinkle of salt. Pour over the remaining cream mixture and bake in the preheated oven for 1–1½ hours, until browned on top. Serve immediately.

COURGETTE GRATIN
WITH FRESH HERBS & GOAT'S CHEESE

This gratin includes a topping of tangy goat's cheese. If you grow your own herbs, add whatever is on offer: majoram, oregano or any other soft-leaved herb, the more the merrier. Simply serve with a mixed salad of lettuce and ripe tomatoes and a big basket of fresh crusty bread.

250 ml/1 cup double/heavy cream
leaves from a small bunch of fresh
    flat-leaf parsley, finely chopped
small bunch of fresh chives, snipped
pinch of grated nutmeg
75 g/2½ oz. Gruyère, grated/shredded
1.5 kg/3¾ lb. courgettes/zucchini,
    very thinly sliced
150 g/5½ oz. soft goat's cheese
salt and black pepper

SERVES 4

Preheat the oven to 190°C (375°F) Gas 5.

Put the cream, parsley, chives, nutmeg, salt and pepper in a small bowl and whisk together. Add half the Gruyère.

Arrange half the courgette slices in a buttered baking dish, sprinkle with the remaining Gruyère and season with a little salt. Top with the remaining courgette slices, season again and pour over the cream mixture. Crumble the goat's cheese over the top.

Bake in the preheated oven for 35–45 minutes until browned. Serve immediately.

NOTE If preferred, you can make the gratin in 4 individual dishes, simply reduce the cooking time by about 5–10 minutes.

MUSHROOM & POTATO GRATIN WITH GRUYÈRE

A luxurious take on a classic potato gratin, given an umami richness by the addition of mushrooms and Gruyère. A great dinner party dish, this is an excellent accompaniment for a rich beef stew.

25 g/1 oz. dried mushrooms
  (a mixture of morels, trompette,
  girolle and porcini)
300 ml/1¼ cups full fat/whole milk
300 ml/1¼ cups double/heavy cream
sprig of fresh thyme
1 garlic clove, chopped
pinch of grated nutmeg
900 g/2 lbs. waxy potatoes, peeled
  and finely sliced
1 tbsp olive oil
1 shallot, finely chopped
250 g/9 oz. fresh white/cup
  mushrooms, thinly sliced
150 g/5 oz. Gruyère, thinly sliced
15 g/1 tbsp butter
salt and black pepper

SERVES 6

Soak the dried mushrooms in hot water for 20 minutes; drain and discard the liquid.

Bring the milk, cream, thyme and garlic to the boil in a pan. Season with salt, freshly ground black pepper and the nutmeg. Add the potato slices and simmer for 10 minutes.

Preheat the oven to 180°C (350°F) Gas 4.

Meanwhile, heat the olive oil in a frying pan/skillet. Add the shallot and fry over low heat, stirring, for 2 minutes, before adding the sliced mushrooms. Increase the heat to high and fry for a further 3 minutes, stirring, until the mushrooms are lightly browned. Add the soaked dried mushrooms. Season with salt and freshly ground black pepper.

In a shallow, ovenproof dish, arrange one-third of the creamy potato mixture in a layer at the bottom of the dish. Top with half of the Gruyère slices and then half the mushroom mixture. Repeat the layers, then finish with the last of the potato mixture. Dot the surface with the butter.

Bake in the preheated oven for 50–60 minutes until golden brown on top. Serve hot from the oven.

SALMON & BROCCOLI GRATIN WITH PESTO

Use a good-quality store-bought fresh pesto for this dish – or make your own.

975 g/2 lb. 2 oz. waxy potatoes, peeled

large head of broccoli (about 480 g/ 1 lb. 1 oz.), separated into florets

400 g/14 oz. boneless, skinless salmon fillet

1 tbsp olive oil

20 g/generous ⅓ cup fresh breadcrumbs

4 tbsp grated/shredded Parmesan

250 ml/1 cup single/light cream

2 tbsp fresh pesto

4 tbsp full-fat/whole milk

30–40 g/2–3 tbsp butter, cut into small pieces

salt and black pepper

SERVES 4–6

Preheat the oven to 200°C (400°F) Gas 6.

Put the potatoes in a large saucepan and add sufficient cold water to cover. Parboil until almost tender when pierced with a knife. Drain. When cool enough to handle, slice into 3 mm/⅛ inch thick rounds.

Bring another pan of water to the boil. Add the broccoli and a pinch of salt and cook for 3–4 minutes until just tender. Drain and let cool. Cut into bite-sized pieces and set aside.

Rub the salmon with the oil and place on a sheet of foil, turned up at the sides to catch any juices, and put it on a baking sheet. Sprinkle with salt. Bake in the oven for 10–15 minutes until cooked through. Let cool, then flake, removing any bones.

In a small bowl, mix together the breadcrumbs and 2 tablespoons of the Parmesan. Season well and set aside. In another bowl, stir together the cream and pesto. Season well and set aside.

To assemble, arrange the potato slices on the bottom of the prepared baking dish in an even layer, sprinkle with salt and the remaining Parmesan, and drizzle with the milk. Arrange the broccoli in an even layer on top of the potatoes and season lightly. Top with the cooked salmon in an even layer.

Pour over the pesto and cream mixture. Sprinkle the breadcrumb mixture over the top and dot with the butter. Bake in the oven for 25–30 minutes until just browned and crisp on top.

CHEESY POLENTA & ROASTED VEGETABLE PIE

Polenta is classic Italian cornmeal, which is cooked into a kind of porridge. For this recipe you need the quick-cook version, as it can be prepared very speedily. It is used here to cover oven-roasted vegetables and topped with melting mozzarella to make a comforting and nutritious pie.

2 small courgettes/zucchini

1 red (bell) pepper

1 yellow (bell) pepper

300 g/10½ oz. broccoli, sliced into long thin 'trees'

1 red onion, sliced into thick rings

2–3 tbsp extra-virgin olive oil

200 g/1⅓ cups quick-cook polenta/cornmeal

15 g/1 tbsp butter

80 g/2¾ oz. Cheddar, grated/ shredded

125-g/4½-oz. mozzarella ball, sliced

salt

MAKES 6–8 SERVINGS

Preheat the oven to 200°C (400°F) Gas 6.

Cut the courgettes in half widthways, then halve lengthwise and cut into long thin fingers. Deseed the (bell) peppers, then cut into thick slices. Spread the vegetables in a single layer on a baking sheet and add the broccoli and onion. Drizzle over the oil and toss to coat. Season lightly with salt.

Roast in the oven for 10–20 minutes until just tender and lightly browned. You may need to roast in batches, depending on the size of your vegetables. The broccoli may cook faster. Check after 15 minutes and remove it if necessary, then continue cooking the other vegetables. Remove from the oven and transfer to a baking dish.

Put 800 ml/3¼ cups water in a large pan, season lightly and add the polenta in a stream. Cook, whisking continuously, until thick. Take care as polenta can bubble up a bit ferociously.

When thick, lower the heat and continue cooking, stirring continuously, for 5 minutes more.

Remove from the heat and stir in the butter and Cheddar. Pour over the vegetables in the dish and spread out with a spatula. Arrange the mozzarella on top and bake in the preheated oven for 25 minutes until browned and bubbling. Serve hot.

CHEESE-TOPPED GNOCCHI BAKE

This is the ultimate mid-week supper. It is quick, filling and delicious. You won't be able to resist the bubbling cheesy top when it comes out of the oven.

700 g/1 lb. 9 oz. gnocchi

680 g/2¾ cups passata/strained tomatoes

handful of sweetcorn/corn kernels

handful of Swiss chard

200 g/7 oz. mozzarella, grated/shredded

handful of breadcrumbs

SERVES 4

Preheat the oven to 180°C (350°F) Gas 4.

Cook the gnocchi in a pan of boiling water as per the package instructions. They are ready when they all bob to the top of the pan.

Drain and put back in the pan (not over the heat) and stir in the passata, sweetcorn and chard. Season.

Pour into a baking dish and sprinkle the mozzarella and breadcrumbs over the top. Bake in the preheated oven for 30–40 minutes or until brown on top.

CHARD, ONION & PARMESAN GRATIN

You may be tempted to discard the fleshy white central rib of chard leaves but they make a delicate-tasting gratin that can be served as a sumptuous side dish or with the addition of crusty bread and some dressed salad as a main meal.

1 tbsp olive oil

30 g/2 tbsp butter

1 onion, roughly chopped

1 tsp finely chopped fresh thyme leaves or ½ tsp dried thyme

stalks from a large bunch of chard, washed, trimmed and sliced, plus 4 chard leaves, roughly shredded

1 tbsp plain/all-purpose flour

150 ml/⅔ cup full-fat/whole milk

1 tbsp crème fraîche or double/heavy cream (optional)

25 g/¾ oz. Grana Padano or Parmesan, grated/shredded, plus 3 tbsp for the topping

2 tbsp fresh breadcrumbs (optional)

salt and black pepper

SERVES 2

Heat a non-stick pan, add the oil and 15 g/1 tablespoon of the butter, and tip in the onion. Cover with a lid and cook over low heat for 5–6 minutes until beginning to soften. Stir in the thyme, then add the chard stalks and cook for another 3–4 minutes. Season.

Preheat the grill/broiler to medium.

Stir the flour into the onion mixture, then add the milk, bring to the boil and simmer until the sauce has thickened. Stir in the chard leaves and cook for 1 minute, then add the crème fraîche and cheese.

Tip into an ovenproof dish. Mix the remaining 3 tablespoons of cheese with the breadcrumbs, if using, and scatter over the gratin. Chop the remaining butter into little pieces and dot over the top. Grill/broil until brown and bubbling.

LOADED POTATO SKINS

Who doesn't like baked potatoes? This is a pimped up, twice-baked, but very simple baked potato. It forms a good opportunity to sort out the dairy items in the fridge! This recipe is vegetarian, but you could add some crispy bacon to the mix if you wish, for a bit of a salty crunch.

2 large baking potatoes
rapeseed/canola oil, for baking
6 spring onions/scallions
150 g/scant ¾ cup full-fat
    cream cheese
about 80 ml/⅓ cup full-fat/whole milk
100 g/½ cup fresh pesto
100 g/3½ oz. cheese (Parmesan,
    Cheddar, Gouda, mozzarella)
salt and black pepper

SERVES 2

Preheat the oven to 230°C (450°F) Gas 8.

Carefully stab the potatoes with a sharp knife, then rub in a little oil and salt. Place on a baking sheet and pop on the top shelf of the preheated oven. Bake for 1½ hours.

About 10 minutes before the potatoes have had their time, trim and slice the spring onions and add to a large mixing bowl with the cream cheese, milk and pesto. Grate in all of the cheese. Season very well and set aside.

Remove the potatoes from the oven. Holding them with a tea/dish towel, cut in half and scoop the flesh straight into the mixing bowl. Roughly mash the ingredients together, then pile back into the skins and place back on the baking sheet.

Return to the oven for 20 minutes until golden, bubbling and ready to devour. Serve immediately.

TIP Feel free to add any herbs, chopped olives or extra bits and bobs (such as cooked ham, bacon, tuna or veg) to the potato filling if you wish.

HAM & EMMENTAL CRÊPES

These thin pancakes are filled, rolled up and then topped with more cheese.

140 g/1 cup plain/all-purpose flour
1 egg and 1 yolk
30 g/2 tbsp melted butter,
    plus extra butter for cooking
2 tsp wholegrain mustard
300 ml/1¼ cups full-fat/whole milk
120 g/1 cup wafer-thin ham
150 g/5½ oz. Emmental,
    grated/shredded
salt and black pepper

BÉCHAMEL
825 ml/3⅓ cups milk
1 small onion, peeled and kept whole
1 tsp black peppercorns
2 bay leaves
pinch of grated nutmeg
75 g/5 tbsp unsalted butter
75 g/⅓ cup plain/all-purpose
    flour, sifted

SERVES 8

For the béchamel, put the milk in a pan over medium heat. Add the onion, peppercorns, bay leaves and nutmeg, and bring to the boil. Remove from the heat. Leave to infuse for 30 minutes. Strain and discard the onion, bay leaves and peppercorns.

In a separate pan, melt the butter until it starts to foam. Tip in the flour in one go, remove the pan from the heat and beat until you have a thick paste that leaves the sides of the pan. Reheat the milk and add it, a little at a time, to the flour paste, beating over the heat until all the milk is incorporated you have a smooth white sauce. Season to taste. Cover and set aside.

To make the crêpe batter, put the flour, egg, egg yolk, melted butter and mustard in a large mixing bowl and season. Add the milk gradually, whisking until you have a smooth batter. Leave to rest in the fridge for 30 minutes, then stir the batter once.

Melt a little butter in a frying pan/skillet over medium heat, then add a ladleful of batter and quickly spread it out thinly. When the top is set, flip it over and cook the other side for 1–2 minutes until golden. Keep warm while you cook the rest.

Preheat the oven to 190°C (375°F) Gas 5.

Spread béchamel over each crêpe, top with some ham and a little cheese, and then roll up. Place in an ovenproof dish and repeat with the remaining crêpes. Pour the rest of the béchamel over the pancakes and top with the remaining cheese. Bake in the oven for 10–15 minutes until the cheese is golden brown.

PASTA, PARMESAN & CHERRY TOMATO PIES

This is a take on the classic Scottish macaroni pie or 'peh'. These are delicious served freshly baked out of the oven – once you've tried cheesy pasta baked in a pastry case you will never look back!

900 g/2 lb. store-bought shortcrust pastry
110 g/4 oz. dried pasta shapes (such as small rigatoni, fusilli, tubetti or macaroni)
40 g/3 tbsp unsalted butter
2½ tbsp plain/all-purpose flour, plus extra for dusting
pinch of cayenne pepper
pinch of English mustard powder
350 ml/1½ cups full-fat/whole milk
100 g/3½ oz. mature/sharp Cheddar, grated/shredded
30 cherry or baby plum tomatoes, halved
50 g/1¾ oz. Parmesan, grated/shredded
salt and black pepper
6 x 10-cm/4-inch straight-sided ramekins, jars, chef's rings or other small pie moulds

MAKES 6

Divide the pastry dough into six pieces. On a lightly floured surface, roll out each piece thinly with a rolling pin. Line each mould with a piece of pastry and smooth gently to fit. Don't worry about uneven edges – these will be trimmed off later. Set on a tray and chill for 30 minutes. When firmly set, use a sharp knife to trim the pastry on each one to 5 cm/2 inches deep.

Preheat the oven to 200°C (400°F) Gas 6.

Cook the pasta according to the package instructions. While the pasta is cooking, melt the butter in a pan and add the flour, cayenne pepper and mustard. Cook, stirring, for 1 minute. Remove from the heat. Pour in the milk and whisk in well. Return to the heat and stir until boiling. Simmer, stirring all the time, for 2 minutes.

Drain the pasta and stir into the sauce. Season to taste and stir in the grated Cheddar. Set aside and leave to cool until tepid.

Spoon the pasta into the pastry cases, leaving enough of a rim of pastry projecting above to hold the tomatoes. Pile the tomato halves over the surface of the pies and sprinkle with the Parmesan. Stand the pies in a shallow baking pan and bake in the preheated oven for 25–30 minutes, or until the filling is golden and bubbling and the pastry is cooked through.

CHEESE & BACON BREAD PUDDING

This is a really satisfying dish that is a meal all on its own. It needs no accompaniment, although you could serve it with a salad if you wish. Rich and creamy, this is the ultimate comfort food on a cold winter's evening.

50 g/3½ tbsp unsalted butter
300 ml/1¼ cups full-fat/whole milk
300 ml/1¼ cups double/heavy cream
180 g/1 cup bacon lardons or thick sliced back bacon, cut into cubes
1 onion, finely chopped
140 g/⅔ cup sweetcorn/corn kernels
5 slices bread (brown or white)
4 eggs, beaten
85 g/3 oz. Cheddar, grated/shredded
salt and black pepper

SERVES 4

Preheat the oven to 180°C (350°F) Gas 4.

Put the butter, milk and cream in a saucepan set over gentle heat, and heat until the butter has melted. Set aside to cool.

Put the bacon lardons in a frying pan/skillet and cook for a few minutes until they have released some oil and are lightly golden brown, then add the onion to the pan and cook until softened. Stir in the sweetcorn and cook for 2–3 minutes.

Cut the bread slices into quarters and arrange a layer over the base of an ovenproof dish. Spoon over a little of the bacon and corn mixture, spread evenly, then add another layer of bread. Continue layering up the bread and filling mixture until all the ingredients are used up.

Season the cooled milk mixture with salt and black pepper, then whisk in the eggs. Pour the mixture over the bread filling and sprinkle the cheese over the top. Bake in the preheated oven for 25–30 minutes until golden brown, and serve.

CHAPTER 4
HOT DIPS & FONDUE

HAWAIIAN-STYLE CHEESE, BACON & PINEAPPLE DIP

This decadent hot dip is made with gooey melted cheese, pineapple and salty pancetta. You can replace the pancetta with ham or fried bacon lardons if you prefer. Or, if pepperoni pizza is your top choice, try swapping the pancetta for pepperoni slices.

100 g/3½ oz. pancetta rashers/slices
4 slices of fresh pineapple
or 4 canned pineapple rings
250 g/9 oz. full-fat cream cheese
125 ml/½ cup Thousand Island dressing
1 tbsp sun-dried tomato purée/paste
100 g/3½ oz. Red Leicester or Colby, grated/shredded
salt and black pepper
tortilla chips or crusty bread, to serve

SERVES 6–8

Preheat the oven to 180°C (350°F) Gas 4.

Chop the strips of pancetta into 2.5-cm/1-inch pieces and put in a roasting pan. If using a fresh pineapple, remove the skin, eyes and hard core, then chop into small pieces. If using canned pineapple, chop the rings into small pieces. Add the pineapple to the roasting pan and bake in the preheated oven for 10 minutes. Remove from the oven and leave to cool slightly. Leave the oven on.

Put the cream cheese in an ovenproof bowl. Add the Thousand Island dressing and tomato purée and whisk together until smooth. Stir in the grated cheese, cooled pancetta and pineapple pieces, and season with salt and pepper. Bake in the oven for 20–25 minutes until golden brown on top.

Leave to cool slightly for about 10 minutes, then serve warm with tortilla chips or crusty bread for dipping.

VARIATION For a Hawaiian 'pizza' dip, try using pepperoni slices instead of the pancetta and arrange them on top of the dip as you would with a pizza. This cute novelty presentation is guaranteed to appeal to kids!

HOT PHILLY CHEESESTEAK DIP

This recipe is inspired by the Philly cheesesteak – a steak sandwich made with thin slices of beef, topped with melting cheese.

1 green (bell) pepper

1 onion, finely chopped

1 tbsp olive oil

1 tsp balsamic glaze or vinegar

1 tsp caster/granulated sugar

6 slices of roast beef

250 g/9 oz. full-fat cream cheese

125 ml/½ cup ranch salad dressing

1 tbsp creamed horseradish

100 g/3½ oz. Provolone or Cheddar, grated/shredded

salt and black pepper

tortilla chips or crusty bread, to serve

SERVES 6–8

Preheat the oven to 180°C (350°F) Gas 4.

Cut away the top of the pepper and discard. Cut the pepper in half, remove all of the seeds, then cut into small chunks about 1 cm/½ inch in diameter. Put the pepper and onion in a large frying pan/skillet with the olive oil and fry over gentle heat until the onion and pepper are soft and the onion starts to caramelize. Drizzle with the balsamic glaze, sprinkle over the caster sugar, season with salt and pepper and fry for a few more minutes.

Cut the roast beef into small pieces and add to the pan. Cook for a minute or so, so that the meat absorbs the flavours from the pan. Remove from the heat and leave to cool for a few minutes.

In an ovenproof bowl, whisk together the cream cheese, ranch dressing and creamed horseradish. Fold the grated cheese into the mixture with the beef and vegetables.

Bake in the preheated oven for 20–25 minutes until the cheese has melted and the top of the dip has started to turn light golden brown. Leave to cool for about 10 minutes before serving, as the dip should be served warm and not hot. Serve with tortilla chips or slices of crusty bread for dipping. Delicious!

VARIATION To make a spicy version, fold in some finely chopped jarred jalapeños with the beef before baking.

HOT BUFFALO CHICKEN & MELTED CHEESE DIP

This dip has the taste of hot buffalo wings but without the bother of getting messy fingers eating actual wings. Hot sauces vary in fierceness, so please do add gradually.

300 g/10½ oz. full-fat cream cheese
170 ml/¾ cup ranch salad dressing
125 ml/½ cup hot sauce
   (such as Frank's)
150 g/5½ oz. Cheddar, grated/
   shredded
200 g/7 oz. cooked chicken breast
freshly ground black pepper
tortilla chips, to serve

SERVES 6–8

Preheat the oven to 180°C (350°F) Gas 4.

Put the cream cheese, ranch dressing and hot sauce in an ovenproof bowl and whisk together until smooth. Stir in the grated cheese. Remove any skin from the chicken breasts and discard, then chop into small pieces and stir into the sauce. Season with cracked black pepper and taste. There should be sufficient salt from the dressing and hot sauce.

Bake in the preheated oven for 25–30 minutes until the top of the dip starts to turn golden. Remove from the heat and leave to cool for a short while then serve warm with tortilla chips.

VARIATION To make a version suitable for vegetarians, simply use a vegetarian cheese and replace the cooked chicken breast with butter/lima beans or small florets of steamed or boiled cauliflower.

250-g/9-oz. Camembert
leaves from 2 sprigs of fresh thyme
2 tbsp runny honey
1 red (bell) pepper, sliced into
 1-cm/½-inch pieces
1 Granny Smith apple, cored and
 sliced into 8 wedges
1 large carrot, cut into 3-cm/1¼-inch
 fingers
sourdough bread, to serve

SERVES 2–4

BAKED HONEY & THYME CAMEMBERT WITH CRUDITÉS

How to make friends and influence people? Serve them this oozing, melted cheese with a selection of chopped vegetables, apple slices and sourdough bread for dipping.

Preheat the oven to 200°C (400°F) Gas 6.

Score the top of the Camembert with a sharp knife, but leave the cheese in the box.

Push the thyme leaves into the scores, then drizzle over the honey.

Replace the lid loosely, and place the box on a baking sheet.

Bake the Camembert in the preheated oven for 20 minutes until the cheese is all melted and wobbles when you move the sheet pan gently.

Serve the Camembert with the pepper, apple and carrot crudités, and sourdough bread.

FONDUTA

The Italian version of fondue is a speciality of the Valle d'Aosta in the north-west. It is made with Fontina cheese, enriched with egg yolks, then scattered decadently with shavings of white truffles from neighbouring Piedmont. If you don't have a truffle, use a sprinkling of truffle oil.

½ tsp cornflour/cornstarch
250 ml/1 cup full-fat/whole milk
500 g/1 lb. 2 oz. Fontina, grated/shredded
50 g/3½ tbsp unsalted butter (optional)
4 egg yolks
freshly ground white pepper
1 white truffle (optional) or truffle oil

TO SERVE
steamed spring vegetables such as baby carrots, baby leeks, baby turnips, asparagus, fennel and mangetout/snow peas, cut into bite-sized pieces if necessary
toast or polenta triangles

SERVES 6

Put the cornflour into a small bowl, add 1 tablespoon of the milk and stir until dissolved – this is called 'slaking'.

Put the remaining milk into the top section of a double boiler, then add the cheese and slaked cornflour. Put over a saucepan of simmering water and heat, stirring continuously, until the cheese melts. Stir in the butter, if using. Remove from the heat.

Put the egg yolks into a bowl and whisk lightly. Whisk in a few tablespoons of the hot cheese mixture to warm the yolks. Pour this mixture back into the double boiler, stirring vigorously. Return the saucepan to the heat and continue stirring until the mixture thickens.

To serve, ladle the cheese mixture into preheated bowls and sprinkle with freshly ground white pepper and shavings of truffle, if using. Alternatively, sprinkle with a few drops of truffle oil. Serve the bowls surrounded by the prepared vegetables, with toast or polenta triangles for dipping.

RACLETTE

The word raclette is the name of a Swiss cheese and the dish you use it for. Raclette cheese is a washed-rind, extremely melty cheese that comes in large wheels. It is melted against a heated element and scraped off using a spatula (the word *racleur* meaning to 'scrape') onto awaiting just-boiled potatoes.

1.2 kg/2 lb. 11 oz. waxy new potatoes
1-kg/2 lb. 4-oz. piece of raclette
gherkins, pickled silverskin onions,
    cured meats and salamis, to serve
salt and black pepper

TOMATO SALAD
6 large vine tomatoes, sliced
1 garlic clove, crushed
1 tbsp red wine vinegar
good pinch of sugar
4 tbsp extra-virgin olive oil
2 tbsp freshly chopped parsley leaves

GREEN SALAD
2 tbsp white wine or cider vinegar
1 tsp Dijon mustard
4 tbsp extra-virgin olive oil
2 tbsp crème fraîche or sour cream
1 large head of soft green lettuce
raclette grill

SERVES 6

Cook the potatoes in boiling salted water until tender. Drain well. Line a bowl with a clean kitchen towel, tip the potatoes into it and wrap them up to keep warm.

Meanwhile, make the salads. For the tomato salad, put the tomatoes on a platter. Whisk the garlic, red wine vinegar, sugar and some seasoning in a small bowl then gradually add the oil. Pour over the tomatoes and scatter with the parsley.

For the green salad, whisk the vinegar and mustard together with plenty of seasoning. Whisk in the oil and crème fraîche. Loosen with a little water if you need to. Wash the lettuce and put in a serving bowl. Pour over the dressing and toss.

Melt the exposed side of the raclette cheese against the grill of a raclette machine. Once melting and bubbling, put a few potatoes on a plate and scrape a layer of the cheesy goodness on top of the potatoes. Repeat for the next plate.

Eat with the salads, cured meats and pickles.

CHEDDAR & CIDER FONDUE

Although the classic fondue recipe is Swiss, it's possible to make it with other cheeses.

270 g/9½ oz. Cheddar, grated/
   shredded
120 g/4 oz. soft ripened farmstead
   cheese, such as Brie or Camembert,
   rind removed
2 tsp cornflour/cornstarch
200 ml/¾ cup dry but fruity hard cider
1 tbsp apple brandy or Calvados
freshly ground white or black pepper
crusty bread, cubed, and apple wedges,
   to serve
fondue pan and burner

SERVES 2–3

Toss the cheeses with the cornflour. Set aside until it has come to room temperature.

Start off the fondue on the hob/stovetop. Pour the cider into a fondue pan and heat until almost boiling. Remove from the heat and tip in about one-third of the cheese. Keep breaking up the cheese with a wooden spoon using a figure of eight motion. (Stirring it round and round as you do with a sauce makes it more likely that the cheese will separate).

Once the cheese has begun to melt, return it to very low heat, stirring continuously. Gradually add the remaining cheese until you have a smooth, thick mass (this takes about 10 minutes, less with practice). If it seems too thick, add some more hot cider. Add the brandy. Season with white pepper.

Place over a fondue burner and serve with the cubes of bread. Use long fondue forks to dip the bread in, stirring the fondue often to prevent it solidifying.

INDEX

RECIPE CREDITS

FIONA BECKETT
Chard, Onion & Parmesan
  Gratin
Cheddar & Cider Fondue
Italian Four-Cheese Pizza

MAXINE CLARK
Pasta, Parmesan & Cherry
  Tomato Pies
Pizza Bianco

MEGAN DAVIES
Loaded Potato Skins
Weekend Quesadillas

ROSS DOBSON
Cauliflower & Gruyere Soup
Mushroom, Fontina,
  Spinach & Potato Bake

TORI HASCHKA
Deep-dish Meatball Pizza Pie

LIZZIE KAMENETZKY
French Onion Soup with
  Comté Toasts
Raclette
Swiss Chard & Gruyere Gratin
Tartiflette

KATHY KORDALIS
Gratin de Chou-Fleur

JENNY LINFORD
Mushroom & Potato Gratin
  with Gruyere

**CLAIRE McDONALD
& LUCY McDONALD**
Cheese-topped gnocchi bake

HANNAH MILES
Brown Butter Baked Potato
  Soup
Cheese & Bacon Bread
  Pudding
Ham & Emmental Crêpes
Hawaiian-style Cheese, Bacon
  & Pineapple Dip
Hot Philly Cheesesteak Dip
Hot Buffalo Chicken & Melted
  Cheese Dip

LOUISE PICKFORD
The Ultimate Grilled Cheese

FIONA SMITH
Fonduta

JENNY TSCHIESCHE
Baked Honey & Thyme
  Camembert with Crudités

**LAURA WASHBURN
HUTTON**
Aubergine Parmigiana
  Mac 'n' Cheese
Baked Rigatoni with
  Mozzarella
Basic Grilled Cheese
BBQ Chicken Mac 'n' Cheese
Brie & Apple-Cranberry
  Toastie
Burger Scamorza
Cheesy Polenta
  & Roasted Vegetable Pie
Cheesy Ravioli Bake with
  Grilled Sweet Peppers
Chicory Gratin with Ham
  & Blue Cheese
Classic Mac 'n' Cheese
Courgette Gratin with Fresh
  Herbs & Goat's Cheese
Ham Hock & Smoked

Mozzarella Pasta Bake
Kimchi & Monterey Jack
  Toastie
Leek & Gruyere Grilled
  Cheese
Mushroom & Fontina Toastie
Mushroom, Tarragon &
  Taleggio Pasta Bake
Pancetta, Gorgonzola &
  Tomato Mac 'n' Cheese
Pasta Bake with Hot Dogs,
  Cheese, Onions & Mustard
Provencal Tomato & Goat's
  Cheese Mac 'n' Cheese
Puttanesca & Mozzarella
  Focaccia
Reblochon, Leek & Bacon
  Pasta Bake
Red Onion Chutney &
  Cheddar Toastie
Roasted Asparagus & Pecorino
  Mac 'n' Cheese
Root Vegetable Gratin
Salmon, Broccoli Gratin with
  Pesto
Serrano Ham, Smoked Paprika
  & Spanish Blue Mac 'n'
  Cheese
Smoked Haddock & Spinach
  Mac 'n' Cheese
Smoky Mac 'n' Cheese with
  Caramelized Onion
Spicy Corn Mac 'n' Cheese
Truffled Mac 'n' Cheese
Welsh Rarebit

BELINDA WILLIAMS
Broccoli & Blue Cheese Soup
Field Mushroom Soup with
  Parmesan, Thyme &
  Pancetta
Spinach & Parmesan Soup
  with Nutmeg & Rosemary

PHOTOGRAPHY CREDITS

MARTIN BRIGDALE *Pages 56,
63, 80, 103.90, 93, 94 and 98.*

PETER CASSIDY *Page 39.*

RICHARD JUNG *Pages 11
and 125.*

MOWIE KAY *Pages 86,
114, 117 and 118.*

ALEX LUCK *Page 18.*

STEVE PAINTER *Pages 1, 2, 3,
6, 12, 13, 14, 20, 23, 24, 28,
33, 34, 37, 38, 42, 44, 45, 47,
48, 50, 52, 55, 59, 60, 64, 69,
70, 73, 74, 81, 106, 109, 113
and 121.*

RITA PLATTS *Pages 40
and 104.*

WILLIAM REAVELL *Page 110.*

NASSIMA ROTHACKER
Pages 17, 83 and 85.

IAN WALLACE *Page 27.*

ISOBEL WELD *Page 79.*

STUART WEST *Page 5.*

KATE WHITTAKER *Pages 89
and 101.*

CLARE WINFIELD *Pages 95,
97, 103 and 124.*